UNDERSTANDING
EMERGING MARKETS

D0928744

UNDERSTANDING EMERGING MARKETS
Building Business BRIC by Brick

Stefano Pelle

Response Books
A division of Sage Publications
New Delhi/Thousand Oaks/London

First published in 2007 by

Response Books
A division of Sage Publications India Pvt Ltd
B-42, Panchsheel Enclave
New Delhi 110 017

Sage Publications Inc
2455 Teller Road
Thousand Oaks
California 91320

Sage Publications Ltd
1 Oliver's Yard
55 City Road
London EC1Y 1SP

Published by Tejeshwar Singh for Response Books, phototypeset in 10/12.5 pt Stone Serif by Star Compugraphics Private Limited, Delhi, and printed at Chaman Enterprises, New Delhi.

Library of Congress Cataloging-in-Publication Data

Pelle, Stefano, 1964–
　　Understanding emerging markets: building business BRIC by brick/Stefano Pelle.
　　　　p.　cm.
　　Includes bibliographical references and index.
1. Developing countries—Economic conditions.　2. Developing countries—Economic policy.　I. Title.

HC59.7.P42　　　338.509172′4—dc22　　　2007　　　2006033884

ISBN: 10: 0-7619-3557-6 (PB)　　　10: 81-7829-716-7 (India-PB)
　　　　　13: 978-0-7619-3557-5 (PB)　13: 978-81-7829-716-3 (India-PB)

Production Team:　　Madhuparna Banerjee, Janaki Srinivasan, Mathew P.J. and Santosh Rawat

To my mother, who has experienced with me the extraordinary changes in the Indian subcontinent at the outset of the 21st century.

CONTENTS

ACKNOWLEDGEMENTS

This book was written, thanks to the experience acquired during several years of work in Asia and Russia. Therefore, my first thanks goes to the company where I have been working since 1998, Perfetti Van Melle, that gave me the opportunity of living in these countries for about eight years, thus getting exposed to very different ways and styles of work, as well as to a large cross section of human behaviour.

More specifically, I would like to thank my colleagues in India, who have largely contributed to the book: first of all Chinoo Sethi, who helped me extensively in giving a readable shape to my thoughts; Abha Kohli, who first read the draft and gave some useful suggestions for better editing; Himani Joshi, who helped in collecting some of the materials; Arun Kumar and Sameer Suneja, who gave some valuable inputs for important parts of the central chapters; Harsh Arora and his team, who as always helped with the legal aspects; my colleagues Huub Sanders in China and Marco Tonolo in Brazil, who provided some interesting examples of their living and working in those countries; my colleague Ramesh Jayaraman in Bangladesh, for providing interesting material for the last chapter as well as for having helped in finding a suitable title;

my friend Massimo Baggi in Moscow, who did the same for Russia. A due thanks also goes to Abhimanyu Ghosh and Aiana Dhillon from Planman Media India, who created the link with Sage India, and within Sage, to Leela Kirloskar, who made the link work.

A word of thanks also to my friend Chiara Letizia and my brother Giampiero, who gave suggestions and encouragement and last but not the least, to my wife Shama, who could bear with me during the weekends spent writing instead of relaxing with her.

I also thank Palgrave Macmillan for granting permission to reproduce three graphs (Different Profiles of Expatriates, Government Influence in Business as Perceived by Western Managers, Class Structures in Development Stages) from the book *Strategies for Asia Pacific* by P. Lasserre, H. Schutte (McMillan Press, 1995, London); The Boston Consulting Group for allowing us to copy and reprint the table, The RDE 100 Span Multiple Industries and Countries from the report, *The New Global Challengers: How 100 Top Companies from Rapidly Developing Economies Are Changing the World* by Marcos Aguiar et al. (May 25, 2006); Sage Publications for granting us permission to reprint the graph, Entry and Negotiation Strategies from the book, *Doing Business in Emerging Markets* by S.T. Cavusgil et al. (Sage Publications, 2002).

The proceeds from the royalty of this book will go towards organizations taking care of underprivileged Indian children. Those interested in making a contribution may contact the author at fenestellapo@yahoo.com

INTRODUCTION

The inferiors revolt to become equals and the equals to become superiors. This is the frame of mind that generates revolutions —Aristotle

Since the beginning of the new millennium, the spectacular growth of some emerging countries has been noticed more and more by the media and the opinion leaders. Western countries seem to have finally realized that places like India and China are not only exotic locations to spend holiday time; they are also extremely promising investment destinations and growing economies with the potential of becoming the engines of world growth for the years to come.

The opportunity of building on the growth of some of the most potential economies has given the inspiration for the word BRIC, coined by Goldman Sachs in 2003 (Goldman Sachs 2003). This acronym puts together four of the countries which have shown, during the last few years, a particularly promising development potential, namely, Brazil, Russia, India and China.

In the following pages, the main statistics of these countries will be compared to those of the current largest world economies and projected onto the next decades to understand what could look like the global economic scenario at that time and the possible implications of this.

The market opportunities existing in the BRIC countries leave little choice to companies operating in the developed world and in need of growth to sustain their profitability but to conquer a significant share of them. An early entry in these countries will secure a competitive advantage which could prove crucial to benefit the growth of their emerging middle classes.

Some of the most common mistakes and important decisions to make when entering these markets are analysed in the course of the book. A detailed study of the working environment will touch upon some important issues concerning the internal resources, their utilization and some of the cultural sensitivities proper to the Emerging Countries (E.Cs). The main external forces impacting the business and some of the ways to successfully interact with them will also be dealt with. Two possible approaches to starting a business in E.Cs will be analysed and their main advantages and disadvantages compared. The key choices concerning the business model and the marketing mix variables will be briefly reviewed, and some of the important managerial and ethical issues to be considered in order to achieve a sustainable development will be mentioned towards the end of the book.

The last chapter will give an overall glance at the consequences of the fast growth of the BRIC countries on the international competitive scenario and at the global geopolitical equilibrium. The emerging Multinational Corporations sprouting from their country of origin are on the verge of becoming global companies, thus taking market share from the established international players.

On a different perspective, the buoyancy of the economies of the E.Cs drastically alters the world geopolitical situation, by increasing the weight of the rising nations that become a stronger counterpart to the current dominance of the USA.

The book is the result of many years of operation in several E.Cs: it focuses therefore, on day-to-day facts and situations rather than on a theoretical perspective, trying to provide useful insights to smoothly overcome hurdles and difficulties to those who have decided to start a business or have already a presence to be developed in one of these countries. However, there are at times recalls and references to Business and Marketing Theories and Manuals, which could be of use to the reader who would like to go more in depth in the specific topic.

Many of the examples quoted will be pertaining to the fast-moving consumer goods (FMCG) industries: therefore, the learning shared will be more applicable to those readers operating in their universe. However, the general parts will provide useful insights also for players of industries out of the FMCG, who have decided to catch some of the business opportunities offered in any of the potential E.Cs.

1

WHAT IS AN EMERGING MARKET?

If winter said 'spring is in my heart' who would believe it?
—K. Gibran

1.1 Main Characteristics

The world keeps changing. Whether the evolution of less developed countries towards a capitalistic model or more in general the often-heard term 'globalization' is to be considered a positive progress for the mankind is debatable. It is, however, a fact that some major events of the last three decades of the twentieth century have given a strong impetus to the change of some of those countries defined at that moment as less developed, who have taken the opportunity to re-think their economic models, change patterns and boost the growth of their GDP.

In the Asian continent, the successful examples of the economic development of countries such as Japan, Hong Kong and Taiwan have pushed closed countries such as China and India to progressively open their economies in the attempt to catch up with the progress of their neighbours. In this direction China has joined the WTO in 2001, causing a major change in the trade flows between East and West. The Middle East and particularly the Gulf countries have based their economic development on the natural wealth of oil, thanks to the higher and higher dependency on this of the Western countries. In the European Block, the fall of communism has provided the opportunity of a radical shift towards an open market model for Russia and the former USSR Republics. The NAFTA Trade Agreement, as well as the gradual control of the inflation gained in the South American countries have helped them increase their economic growth and gain a more relevant share of the international trade. All the above, together with the quantum jump experimented in the mass communication technology and, more recently, the spread of mass accessible microprocessors and the Internet, have dramatically accelerated the pace of the changes happening in the world scenario.

In this changed panorama, the economic and political weight of a continent such as Asia has become much larger vis-à-vis only a few decades ago; the Middle East countries have become a strategic gateway between Europe and Asia, as well as a vital source of energy for most of the developed and developing economies; the former Soviet block is more and more integrated to Europe and enjoys the role of an important oil exporter, and the South American countries are playing a relevant role within the WTO. More specifically, countries that used to be classified as less developed or semi-industrialized have started to reinforce their economies and gain importance as trade partners, recipients of foreign investments and political players within the transnational institutions. Such countries are those which we refer to as 'Emerging Markets' (E.Ms).[1]

A few economic indicators would have similar values across these countries: a relatively high GDP growth (more than 5 per cent) but a low per capita GDP (less than 5000 USD/year) would be coupled with a relatively high inflation rate (more than 5 per cent) and a low saving rate. We are therefore, talking about high growth economies in developing countries: however, it will be useful to highlight the differences in definition which are sometimes used as interchangeable, i.e., fast growing, developing and Emerging Countries (E.Cs).

While the first category includes all those countries with a relatively high rate of growth as defined earlier, the second will only comprise those countries whose growth is accompanied to a general improvement of the living conditions; the third category will comprise those countries whose growth and conditions improvement happen in a sustainable way thanks to the conscious effort to bridge the gap with the world's more developed countries. Therefore, we can reasonably state that all E.Cs are both developing and growing; similarly, all developing countries would also be growing; on the other hand, not all fast growing countries would also be developing and not all developing ones would also be emerging.

Several international bodies (World Bank, United Nations, etc.) and magazines (*Economist*) have created a list of 24 leading E.Cs (25 as per the Economist). It is estimated that well over 50 per cent of the world population lives in the same, that they will achieve a growth rate of more than 6 per cent per year during the next two decades and that their share of the world trade would reach almost 27 per cent by 2010 (Cavusgil, Ghauri and Agarwal 2002). By the same date their total GDP is expected to be 50 per cent of that of the industrialized world and the amount of foreign investments flowing in them will be many times more than (almost ten times) what it used to be only 20 years before (almost USD 65 billion).

These few figures are sufficient to give an idea of the huge potential of the E.Ms and explain the reasons of the changed attitude of the investors vis-à-vis them. Less than 20 years ago, they used to look at them with apprehension, underestimating their (market) potentials, also due to the scarcity of available data, the difficulties created by the local laws, and the lack of infrastructures would be considered too big hurdles compared to the limited return the investors would be able to get out of their financial effort.

However, the work undertaken by consulting firms, banks and other professional organizations has helped disclose most of the useful information necessary to understand the fundamentals of the markets and evaluate the potential return on the investments. Governments have become much more cooperative in dealing with prospective investors, reducing the long procedures for the approval and licenses required, and clarifying the processes necessary to enter the country for the expatriates and for the incoming capitals. They have also started to improve the infrastructure of the countries and sometimes to offer fiscal incentives to the prospective investors. The spread of English as the international language and the communication and information revolution brought by the most recent technological innovation have completed the scenario.

Today E.Cs are the priority number one in the list of the developed countries; they represent their future growth, but also their sources of imports, both at raw material and finished goods level; at the same time they are becoming their competitors, initially with cheaper prices, but progressively with better technology and quality coupled with lower prices.

No developed country today can afford to be indifferent to what is happening in the E.Ms. A renowned international magazine interviewed at the end of 2005 the then finance minister of one of the G7 countries. The excerpts here summarizes some of the relevant parts of the interview and provides an idea of the changed perspective that those countries are currently facing (see Box 1.1).

Box 1.1 SALIENT POINTS OF AN INTERVIEW WITH THE ITALIAN FINANCE MINISTER GIULIO TREMONTI

Replying to the question on how European Leaders could face the trading advantage that China and other emerging Asian economic powers possessed, the Minister stated that he was not against the Chinese, since they looked out for their own interests and Europe should simply do the same. Once the world has been opened, one cannot turn around. Europe for too long hasn't protected its economic interests and doesn't have any real industrial policy, nor a strategy for attracting capital. It has too many rules and regulations on businesses coming from Brussels, yet it is freely importing from countries that do not have any of these rules.

A subsequent question sought the meaning of a statement of the Minister, where he had said that the World Trade Organization is a Pandora's Box for Europe. He explained that

(Box 1.1—continued)

(*Box 1.1—continued*)

the opening of the world to free trade had happened too fast and was too intense. From 1994 to 2001, the world trade had (rapidly) opened up and in December 2001, when China entered the WTO, it had all multiplied even further. Japan after World War II, for example, had been brought into world markets gradually, over the course of 30 or 40 years. Europe didn't enter globalization, but globalization entered into Europe, that had found itself unprepared.

The last question touched upon the direct impact of the effects of China's economic boom on Italy. In his opinion Italy is particularly vulnerable because much of industrial production comes from mid-level to relatively low technology, and also because of the high cost of labour. Furthermore, the repeated devaluation of the lira to the overvalued euro had been a shock for the Italian economy.

1.2 The BRIC Countries

The eighteenth and nineteenth centuries saw the European industrial countries conquering overseas nations, sometimes through initial trade relationships, in order to exploit the local resources and increase the wealth and power of the homelands. Thanks to these conquers, but also thanks to the European Industrial Revolution, the share of the global GDP of the so-called developed economies managed to overtake one of the Emerging Economies, which had dominated the world in the previous centuries (see Figure 1.1).

The twentieth century witnessed the end of the colonialist age. However, most of the European countries

FIGURE 1.1 EMERGING COUNTRIES COMING BACK

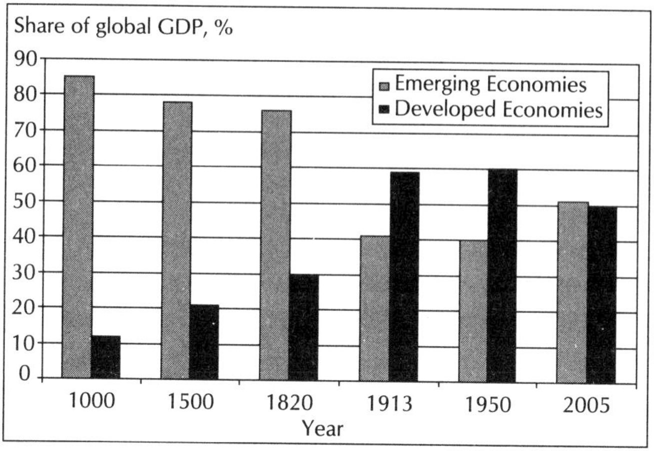

Source: OECD, Angus Maddison, as appeared in *Internazionale*, December 2005.

maintained at least the trade links with the former colonies. The twenty-first century is likely to see a phenomenon which could become a kind of reverse colonialism: some of the formerly dominated countries are likely to become the dominators of a more and more global economy. The process had actually already happened in the previous century with the raising of the USA to the rank of the world's largest economic and military power, but will see a strong acceleration during the coming decades.

Some of the E.Cs have, in fact, been sending their goods, services and people to the industrialized Western ones and have thus subtly started dominating by creating a larger and larger dependence of the same upon the goods imported and the services received.

There are a few countries which, due to different reasons, appear to have the potential to lead the world economy in a few years from now. These countries were studied and brought to the attention of the public through a report released by Goldman Sachs (2003). The research predicted a quantum change within the global economic power, with countries like Brazil, Russia, India and China gaining progressive importance and eventually becoming four of the six largest world economies. Some data contained in the mentioned report can help understand where these countries are today, where they might be tomorrow in the global scenario and what consequences could such a change bring.

The four countries today represent more than 40 per cent of the world's population: since two of these countries, namely India and Brazil, have still a birth rate higher than the average world rate, their numerical weight on the globe's population will not drastically decrease during the years to come. Today the share of the economies of these markets in the global capital market is approximately 3.5 per cent; their per capita incomes range from about 500 USD to 4,500 USD; their total weight in the world economy is approximately 10 per cent. However, their average annual GDP growth exceeds 6 per cent (against a world average of 3.7 per cent, and a much lower rate in the G6 countries) and is projected to remain at this level for many years from now. Thanks to this, their share of the world growth would double during the next 20 years, from 20 to 40 per cent. The per capita income should range in the same period between 2,300 and 16,600 USD, thus becoming four times of what they are now; their weight in the world economy should double to 20 per cent and the share of the world capital market could exceed 15 per cent.

Going still further ahead in time, it is projected that by 2050, China will become the largest world economy, and India will be the third one, not too far away from the USA; Japan will still occupy the fourth position, but very closely followed by Brazil and Russia (see Table 1.1). At that moment, the BRIC countries would have become four of the six largest world economies and all the European members of the G6 would significantly be outpaced.

The study did mention some conditions necessary to ensure that their projected scenario would actually happen: among these were the presence in the countries of stable macroeconomic backgrounds, strong and stable political institutions, openness to trade and foreign direct investments and higher level of educations. We are aware that some of these conditions are not fully

TABLE 1.1 BRIC COUNTRIES' ECONOMIC MAGNITUDE
IN RELATION TO G7

	2003		2050 (Goldman Sachs)	
Ranking	Country (GDP in billion dollars, current prices)		Country (GDP in billion dollars, current prices)	
1	USA	(10,882)	China	(44,453)
2	Japan	(4,326)	USA	(35,165)
3	Germany	(2,401)	India	(27,803)
4	UK	(1,795)	Japan	(6,673)
5	France	(1,748)	Brazil	(6,074)
6	Italy	(1,466)	Russia	(5,870)
7	China	(1,410)	UK	(3,782)
8	Canada	(834)	Germany	(3,603)
9	India	(599)	France	(3,148)
10	Brazil	(492)	Italy	(2,061)
11	Russia	(433)		

Source: WDI database and Goldman Sachs, 2003.

Note: In Goldman Sachs (2003) the basis for comparison is G6, and therefore Canada is not included in the projections for 2050.

in place today in all BRIC countries (e.g., the weak Bank system in China and the potential social conflict there, as well as the possible conflicts with Taiwan or other neighbouring countries); however, despite this, the first years after the study have seen even better results than those projected, as mentioned later in this section.

Such a scenario is based on the assumption of the sustainability of the growth as well as the strong appreciation of the currencies of the BRIC countries. There are therefore chances that reality will sensibly differ from the projections (see Tables 1.2–1.5). However, even

TABLE 1.2 PROJECTED REAL GDP GROWTH OF THE BRIC COUNTRIES

% yoy	Brazil	China	India	Russia
2000	4.2	8.0	5.4	10.0
2005	4.2	7.9	6.2	5.8
2010	4.2	6.6	6.1	4.1
2020	3.7	5.0	5.5	3.3
2030	3.9	3.9	6.1	3.4
2040	3.6	3.7	5.8	2.4
2050	3.4	2.7	5.1	2.1

Source: Goldman Sachs, *BRICs Model Projections,* https://www.gs.com

TABLE 1.3 PROJECTED REAL GDP GROWTH OF THE G6* COUNTRIES

% yoy	France	Germany	Italy	Japan	UK	US
2000	4.2	2.9	3.3	2.8	3.1	3.8
2005	2.3	2.3	2.0	1.4	2.4	3.1
2010	1.6	1.5	1.6	0.6	2.2	2.4
2020	1.7	0.9	1.3	1.4	1.7	2.1
2030	1.5	0.9	0.5	0.6	1.6	2.5
2040	1.7	1.5	1.2	0.7	1.8	2.6
2050	1.7	1.2	1.5	1.3	1.5	2.5

Source: BRICs Model Projections, https://www.gs.com
*Indicative projections made only on the model assumptions described in the text, not G6 official forecasts.

TABLE 1.4 PROJECTED GDP PER CAPITA (IN USD)

Year	BRICs				G6					
	Brazil	China	India	Russia	France	Germany	Italy	Japan	UK	US
2000	4,338	854	468	2,675	22,078	22,814	18,677	32,960	24,142	34,797
2005	2,512	1,324	559	3,718	24,547	24,402	21,277	34,744	27,920	39,552
2010	3,417	2,233	804	5,948	26,314	26,877	23,018	36,172	30,611	42,926
2020	6,302	4,965	1,622	12,527	30,723	31,000	27,239	42,359	36,234	48,849
2030	9,823	9,809	3,473	22,427	35,876	33,898	30,177	49,944	41,194	57,263
2040	16,370	18,209	8,124	35,314	42,601	40,966	33,583	55,721	49,658	69,431
2050	26,592	31,357	17,366	49,646	51,594	48,952	40,901	66,805	59,122	83,710

TABLE 1.5 PROJECTED GDP OF BRIC (IN USD BN)

| Year | BRICs | | | |
	Brazil	China	India	Russia
2000	762	1,078	469	391
2005	468	1,724	604	534
2010	668	2,998	929	847
2020	1,333	7,070	2,104	1,741
2030	2,189	14,312	4,935	2,980
2040	3,740	26,439	12,367	4,467
2050	6,074	44,453	27,803	5,870

PROJECTED GDP OF G6 COUNTRIES (IN USD BN)

| Year | G6 | | | | | | BRICs | G6 |
	France	Germany	Italy	Japan	UK	US		
2000	1,311	1,875	1,078	4,176	1,437	9,825	2,700	19,702
2005	1,489	2,011	1,236	4,427	1,688	11,697	3,330	22,548
2010	1,622	2,212	1,337	4,601	1,876	13,271	5,442	24,919
2020	1,930	2,524	1,553	5,221	2,285	16,415	12,248	29,928
2030	2,267	2,697	1,671	5,810	2,649	20,833	24,416	35,927
2040	2,668	3,147	1,788	6,039	3,201	27,229	47,013	44,072
2050	3,148	3,603	2,061	6,673	3,782	35,165	84,200	54,432

Source: Goldman Sachs, 2006.

if the forecasts will be only partially met, the implications for the world economy will certainly be large. The differential of growth and return on the invested capitals will attract more and more investment in the countries, thus causing currencies' appreciation. The growing wealth in the BRIC will increase their purchasing power, thus the salaries and prices will go up. The local consumption patterns will shift and the upgraded demand will attract global players, who will find in these markets increased opportunities. On the other hand, most of the countries of the G7 will experience reduced growth, loss of employment and possibly lower consumptions, savings and investments.

For the companies who need to maintain acceptable rates of growth, investing in these countries will become mandatory. With such a perspective, long-sighted companies might consider to move their first steps in these markets at the earliest in order to ensure a share of them before competition becomes too fierce.

By the end of 2005 Goldman Sachs had updated their projections and had, at the same time, started looking with deeper focus onto another possible broader group of candidates to be BRIC-like. These were called N-11, i.e., The Next 11 (see Table 1.6), and comprised a group of 11 countries among which some were estimated to have the potential to rival the BRIC economies, namely Mexico and Korea, initially not included in the BRIC report since they had been considered already more

TABLE 1.6 THE N-11 SNAPSHOT

	Population in 2005 (million)	GDP in 2005 (billion USD)	5y Average GDP per cent growth rate (2000–2005)	2005 GDP per capita (USD)
Bangladesh	144	61	5.4	422
Egypt	78	91	4.0	1,170
Indonesia	242	272	4.6	1,122
Iran	68	203	5.7	2,989
Korea	49	814	5.2	16,741
Mexico	106	753	2.6	7,092
Nigeria	129	94	5.1	733
Pakistan	162	120	4.1	737
Philippines	88	98	4.7	1,115
Turkey	70	349	4.3	5,013
Vietnam	84	47	7.2	566

Source: Goldman Sachs, 2006.

developed. This group included countries with large population, since '...without a substantial population even a successful growth story is unlikely to have a global impact' (Goldman Sachs 2006).

The outcome of the new projections, which considered the fact that each of the BRIC countries exceeded the foreseen growth by at least a percentage point during the two years (2004 and 2005) following the original projections, was, for some countries even more optimistic than the one contained in the report of 2003. The highlights of this (see Figures 1.2 and 1.3) was that China would overtake US by 2040, thus a few years before what initially foreseen, whereas India would overtake Japan only in 2033, therefore later than expected, in the light of the recent improvement of the Japanese economy.

If the composite projections (including the N-11) were considered, by that date China would have still become the largest economy, followed by US, India, Japan and Brazil. Mexico however would be slightly ahead of Russia.

Indonesia, Nigeria and Korea could have overtaken Italy and Canada by the same date. In terms of per capita income, by that moment Korea would have a higher income than all the G7 countries (including Canada), except for the US. Also by that date, all of the BRICs and seven of the N-11 would have crossed the USD 15,000 income threshold.

1.3 Market Opportunities

While defining the salient characteristics of the emerging markets, we noticed as common features of many

FIGURE 1.2 THE LARGEST ECONOMIES IN 2050 (USD BILLION)

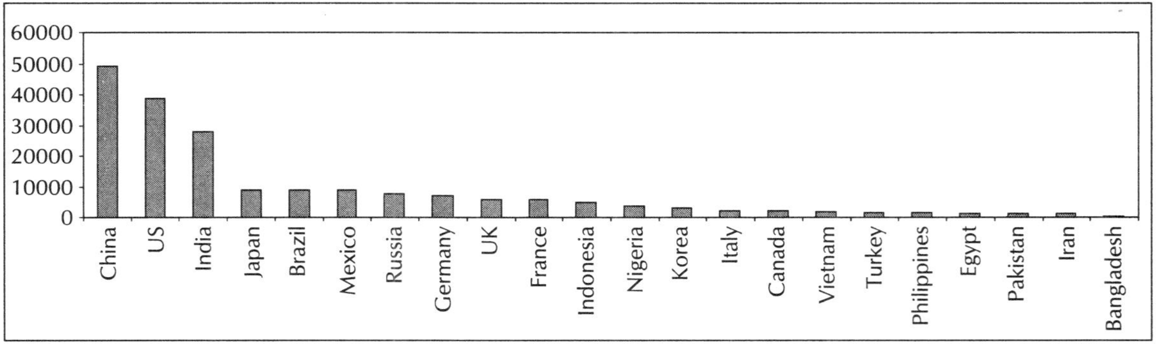

Source: Goldman Sachs, 2006.

TABLE 1.7 INCOME DISTRIBUTION AND MEASURES OF INEQUALITY

	Share of total income or consumption			Richest 10% compared to the poorest 10%[2]	Share of population[3] under 1 dollar	Share of population[4] under 2 dollars	Gini co-efficient[5]
	10% poorest	20% poorest	10% richest				
Brazil	0.7	2.2	48.0	65.8	8.2	22.4	58.5
Russia	1.8	4.9	36.0	20.3	6.1	23.8	45.6
India	3.5	8.1	33.5	9.5	41.8	88.4	32.5
China	2.4	5.9	30.4	12.7	26.5	71.0	44.7
Japan	4.8	10.6	21.7	4.5	–	–	24.9
Denmark	2.6	8.3	21.3	8.1	–	–	24.7

Source: UNDP Human Development Report, 2003 and WDI database, World Bank.

Note: As the underlying random samples vary from country to country in terms of method, data collection and time of compilation, a direct comparison between countries is not possible.

of these the high growth of the GDP, as well as relatively low level of per capita GDP.

Very often, together with these traits a study of the wealth concentration in these countries will also reveal that a small percentage of the population would hold a very large part of the economic resources, thus making the gap between the rich and the poor people quite dramatic (see Table 1.7). These factors constitute the causes of the market opportunities and the distinguishing features of the same.

A large part of the population with low income will represent an important reserve of cheap work force. On the other hand, a high concentration of wealth in the upper layer of the social structure of a liberalized economy should become the basis of a capitalistic approach to the market, since the surplus wealth could be invested in the creation of a manufacturing sector that can avail of low production costs. Investments in industries, as well as in building the infrastructures which will support the industries, will generate new wealth and consequently, increase the per capita income and the GDP growth. The more the ruling governments are able to ensure that part of the wealth generated is fairly distributed among those who participate in the process, the faster will be the economic development of the country, fed by the virtuous circle investments–consumptions–savings–reinvestments. This would represent a favourable framework for those who intend to invest in the countries and cater to the local markets in order to exploit the increasing purchasing power of the same.

However, a foreign company that decides to enter an emerging country might see some different potentials other than selling its goods and services to the local

TABLE 1.7 INCOME DISTRIBUTION AND MEASURES OF INEQUALITY

	Share of total income or consumption			Richest 10% compared to the poorest 10%[2]	Share of population[3] under 1 dollar	Share of population[4] under 2 dollars	Gini co-efficient[5]
	10% poorest	20% poorest	10% richest				
Brazil	0.7	2.2	48.0	65.8	8.2	22.4	58.5
Russia	1.8	4.9	36.0	20.3	6.1	23.8	45.6
India	3.5	8.1	33.5	9.5	41.8	88.4	32.5
China	2.4	5.9	30.4	12.7	26.5	71.0	44.7
Japan	4.8	10.6	21.7	4.5	–	–	24.9
Denmark	2.6	8.3	21.3	8.1	–	–	24.7

Source: UNDP Human Development Report, 2003 and WDI database, World Bank.

Note: As the underlying random samples vary from country to country in terms of method, data collection and time of compilation, a direct comparison between countries is not possible.

population: the local investment could be envisaged to become a manufacturing platform in order to export to other countries, in the light of the availability of raw materials or skilled labour at accessible prices or thanks to special laws and regulations offering attractive incentives for exporters. A combination of these options is the choice of a country which is attractive thanks to the abundance of the raw material/skilled labour that the investing company needs with the objective of competing both in the local market as well as the export markets.

A further possibility is to look at an emerging country as a source of semi-finished goods to be purchased and partially processed locally to be later sent to the country of origin of the investor, where the last finishing is done and the product is made ready to the final consumer. In this case, a relatively small office is set up in the country, equipped with experts in selecting the goods as well as buying. This is the case for some international retailer chains who have established purchasing bases in India. A similar approach is also followed for recruiting local talent to be trained and sent to another country. While this is normally done for high skilled people (IT experts, engineers) by MNCs, there are also cases of export of basic manpower to countries in need of it (e.g., Bangladesh workers brought to the Gulf countries): this last case is normally carried out by local companies, often exporters of goods who decide to diversify their business.

The investment to build an exporting base is normally easier and faster to execute: as a matter of fact, exporters buy foreign currency, and foreign reserves are often scarce in emerging economies. Second, pure exporters do not compete with local producers who could otherwise lobby with the local government in order to create hurdles for the new-comers, thus keeping the market as protected as possible. Furthermore, many of the E.Cs were, up to some years ago (and some are still today), almost closed economies: often exporters also act as importers, thus granting the supply of some of the goods which in the past were or still now are difficult to find.

However, there are some specific difficulties which exporters could face for the nature of their business. Since they deal with foreign currencies, they might run higher risks of losses on exchange without adequate hedging measures, considering the high volatility proper to the currencies in the E.Cs. They also need good transport as well as other communication infrastructure, which are usually not well developed and functioning in those countries. They would have to certainly deal with the custom authorities and be subjected to the local import/export policies, which often change overnight in such countries. Also, it is widely known that customs procedures are the most complicated and full of bureaucratic hurdles, thus, not by chance, customs officers are usually not among the most transparent and helpful categories. (This is also true for developed countries.)

For the time being, we shall not deal with the difficulties faced by the manufacturers, who have decided to operate in the E.Cs, since these will be detailed in the chapter on the working environment: we shall only anticipate that their life would certainly be more complicated than that of the exporters, if not for else due to the resistance that they might face from the local competitors already present, as well as the potential ones.

1.4 The Emerging Middle Class

The socio-economic structure of a country is in continuous evolution: demographic and economic factors as well as migratory movements constitute the main change drivers for them. Extraordinary events (wars, natural disasters) may contribute to accelerate the changes of the same, which would otherwise take several decades to modify their basic trends.

A graphic representation of a country society at a given point of time could be given through the size of the different socio-economic indicators (e.g., per capita income), or by sociological or psychological ones (habits, education, etc.).

Considering the per capita income as the main parameter of differentiation, a less developed country will be graphically represented by a sort of pyramid, where the very large base will represent the majority of the population with a low per capita income and the narrow apex will depict the limited number of rich people. A narrow central section of the pyramid will represent a small middle class; such is often the case of the less developed economies.

At the moment of the first BRIC report, a middle class of more than 250 million was estimated in the four countries, the definition of it being an income of over 3,000 USD per year. While we are writing, the size of the same will have probably crossed 400 million, and would be rapidly growing towards the number estimated by Goldman Sachs for the year 2013: 800 million. If the forecast holds true, by that date the BRIC countries will have a total middle class size larger than the population of Western Europe, USA and Japan combined. They will therefore mature into what Lasserre and Schutte (1995) define as Newly Industrialized Economies, an intermediate step towards becoming developed countries; here the size of the middle class exceeds by far in number that of the other socio-economic clusters (diamond shape) (see Figure 1.4).

FIGURE 1.4 CLASS STRUCTURES IN DEVELOPMENT STAGES

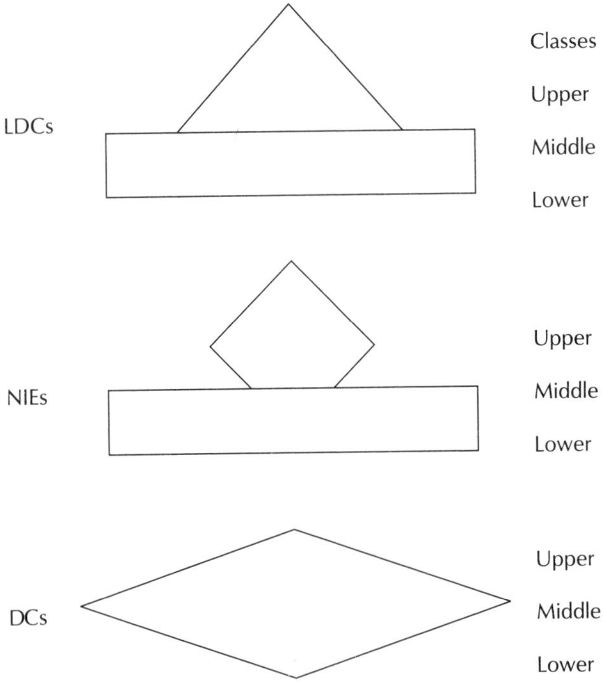

Source: Lasserre and Schutte (1995).

The Emerging Middle Classes (EMCs) have across countries, similar characteristics that marketers will have to analyse and consider while designing and positioning their products. They will contain within themselves a combination of sub-clusters, where the traditional ones, the backbone of the middle class, will be more savings-oriented, more price-conscious and less open to innovations and foreign cultures. Here the income not saved is mainly utilized to purchase daily necessities, mostly food and clothes. Occasionally, part of the savings is invested in the purchase of rather cheap economic durables. People belonging to this sub-cluster would typically live in suburban areas, small towns or in the countryside. They would be loyal to local customs, habits and consumption patterns, therefore likely to buy generic and unbranded products or local brands. Such a sub-cluster would then not be particularly interesting for the MNC marketing its product in an E.C., since its members would not be likely to become consumers of their products in the short term, or possibly not even during the course of their lives.

However, within the EMCs there will also be a completely different kind of sub-cluster, the members of which would instead constitute one of the main target group for companies operating in E.Cs, particularly for those in the consumer durables and in the FMCG sector.

Consumers of this group are those who have benefited from the economic growth of the recent years and represent therefore a transition segment (Lasserre and Schutte 1995). They like to experiment, are open-minded and aspire to reach as close as possible to the upper segment of the societies. They enjoy spending rather than accumulating savings for the future: they would not mind to avail of loans[6] in order to buy a car or a house. Most of this segment is comprised of people between 25 to 40 years of age, a working class living in a world completely different from their parents, possessing education and technical skills allowing them to progressively build up their own economic and social status. Their income is above the average of the total middle class and their consumption patterns are very different from those of the traditional sub-cluster. The percentage of what they spend on food is reduced; the one on household items is constant, but other spending such as travel or insurance increase significantly. The demand for non-essential items, which contribute to increasing the quality of their life, becomes a relevant part of their purchases, growing according to their income. Such people would have moved to urban areas some years earlier and would normally be ready to relocate for work opportunities. As they move from place to place and from job to job, they also rapidly switch from one brand to another. Their 'hunger' for consumer goods and a better quality of life is a consequence of the environment where they have lived: a lower class family of a country, with a closed economy, where local brands would dominate the market scenario.

This was the case in many of the E.Ms, including the BRIC ones, only a few decades (or sometimes even years) ago. Many of these countries up to the eighties (others to the nineties, some till today) had governments and policies which would protect local industries with high duties and other import restrictions, and consequently, the presence of international and global brands was extremely limited.

With the spreading of the mass media and the communication revolution (mobile and technology), the potential demand for the products available in Western countries would at times be starved by the said restrictions: middle class consumers of E.C. would have to rely on relatives visiting from abroad or sometimes the black market to be able to consume the brands they would have seen in television or through some better-off friends.

With the opening of the countries to initially import and later to foreign investors manufacturing locally the international brands, the hunger of the past year has rapidly become a large demand for the same, whenever they were made available with an appropriate marketing mix.

Let us take the example of China to understand better the characteristics of these emerging middle classes.

While still today the country remains a communist regime, the growing of the economy during the seventies has progressively caused a dramatic change in the society, particularly for those clusters living in the urban and coastal areas. Such transformation seems bound to radically change also the political situation of the country a few years ahead.

Reforms in the agricultural sector initially and later, during the mid-eighties, in the industrial one, in combination with the creation of special economic zones opened to foreign investments, have given a strong impulse to the growth of the economy, the acquisition of know-how and technological expertise and the reduction of the influence of the State's centralized administration. As a consequence of this the standard of living has improved very rapidly and so has the per capita income, also due to the one child policy that has limited the overall growth of the population[7] (see Figure 1.5).

Till a few years ago the communist ideology had ensured that the income differential among different levels of the society be minimized (a doctor and an unskilled worker would not have dramatically dissimilar salaries). Today the growing industrial and trading middle class, particularly in some areas of the country,[8]

FIGURE 1.5 THE CONSEQUENCES OF ONE CHILD POLICY IN CHINA

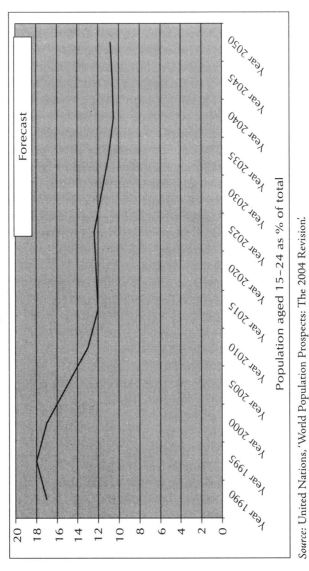

Population aged 15–24 as % of total

Source: United Nations, 'World Population Prospects: The 2004 Revision.'

would have an income manifold that of the average Chinese. However, this cluster, would probably not reach 15 per cent of the total population, though in terms of PPP (Purchasing Power Parity), it had been estimated to have crossed the 300 million already in the late nineties (Prahalad and Lieberthal 1998).

Chinese growing middle class have surprised the whole world for their high level of consumption and 'willingness to accept higher prices in exchange for better product presentation and quality' (Lasserre and Schutte 1995). In spite of a still relatively low average per capita income, the purchasing power of China has been proven to be grossly underestimated, due to the high state subsidies for health, education, housing and infrastructural services in general.

It is therefore rather clear that with the higher level of sophistication of the Chinese middle class, small local producers of average unbranded items will have a hard life, unless they decide to improve their standards to match the international producers' quality (which they seem to be capable of doing!). Till this happens, a market like China represents a source of immense opportunities for international companies targeting a middle class which will soon be comparable to the population of the United States.

Though each E.M. will have middle classes with specific characteristics, the general trend experienced in China is likely to be taking place in a more or less similar way in the rest of the BRIC countries and in many other emerging ones.

Notes

1. This is a definition coined by a member of the World Bank, Antonio W. Van Agtomes, in 1981.

2. The ratio between income or consumption in the richest group compared to the poorest.
3. Share of population subsisting on less than 1 dollar (PPP) per day.
4. Ibid.
5. Gini coefficient indicates the share of income to be redistributed in order to create complete equality in income distribution. A Gini coefficient of zero entails that all have exactly the same income, while a capital coefficient of 100 means that all income goes to one single person.
6. Often in E.Cs loans are one of the retention tools used by the companies and therefore, are very commonly conceded to the employees. According to their level, companies may give white goods schemes, vehicle loans or even long term house loans (usually for Managers).
7. The Chinese Government, in order to contain the growth of the rising population in a closed and aspiring self sufficient country, has imposed a heavy tax burden on families with more than one child. Such law, enforced particularly in urban areas, has completely changed not only the economic but also the social structure of the Chinese society.
8. For example, Shanghai or the Guangdong province.

References

Cavusgil, S.T., P. Ghauri and M. Agarwal. 2002. *Doing Business in Emerging Markets*, New Delhi: Sage Publications.

Lasserre, P. and H. Schutte. 1995. *Strategies for Asia Pacific,* London: McMillan Press.

Prahalad, C.K. and K. Lieberthal. 1998. 'The End of Corporate Imperialism', *Harvard Business Review*.

Sachs, Goldman. 2003. *Dreaming with BRICs: The Path to 2050.* https://www.gs.com

———. 2006. *The World and the BRICs Dream*. New York: Goldman Sachs.

———. *BRICs Model Projections*. https://www.gs.com

2

To conquer the future one has to first dream about it
—B. Pascal

2.1 Common Mistakes

Any strategic investment decision is normally based on a business plan. This analyses the work environment and summarises the findings in a background, states some objectives, commits resources to achieve the same and foresees a certain return on the investment within a time-frame based on the assumptions considered.

The decision of investing in an E.M. (emerging market) would also typically follow the same pattern and, according to the finding of the preliminary market studies, will select one or more country where to enter and proceed in the implementation of the strategies selected in order to achieve the objective fixed.

A number of variables can influence the result of the business plan: we shall analyse what can go wrong in the whole process by considering separately the stage of the preparation of the plan, which we shall call the desk work, and that of the actual implementation of the same, which we shall call the action phase.

The former comprises of a market study, the analysis of the findings and the extrapolation of the same into some assumptions, the determination of some objectives and the selection of the adequate strategies to achieve these. The latter comprises of the activities carried out in line with the strategies, the analysis of the results and the fine tuning of the strategies (and sometimes also of the objectives) in the light of actual market experiences.

The desk work starts with the market research: a critical element of this is the brief given to the research firm. In a developed market, in case of the launch of a new product in an FMCG industry, the emphasis of the study will be on the existing consumers; in an E.M., such an approach could give deceptive results, particularly when the product represents a novelty, thus the current consumption is clearly limited. In this case the stress should go on the prospective new consumers, those using similar categories which could be substituted with the new product and could possibly shift to the new category. Even in the case of a product category already present in the market, due to a number of reasons later analysed, one would probably find out that the socio-economic clusters consuming the products in an E.M. will be different from those consuming the same in the market where these were originally launched.[1] This clearly indicates that a wrong research brief could lead to wrong findings, thus suggesting unrealistic objectives and affecting the whole business plan.

The analysis of the findings and the extrapolation of the assumptions could also be completely misleading. It might happen (and often it does) that instead of hypothesis-based research data, one would read the data with preconceived assumptions, thus finding opportunities which do not exist or missing some others which could be very potential. Often the wrong assumptions are the consequences of the belief that a successful model in the country of origin could be easily replicated with minimal changes in an E.M. An example of this is the launch of the Fiat Palio in Brazil, a good success obtained in the mid nineties which Fiat attempted to replicate in India a few years later. It is interesting to notice that in this case, the model was exported from one E.M. to another, thus the chances of success on paper could have been higher than in a case of a model exported from a developed market to an emerging one. After a few months of initial success, the sales of the car dropped dramatically: possible explanations could be found in the petrol consumptions, which has considered to be too high in India, as well as the absence of an after-sales infrastructure, which created long delays in the maintenance and repairing of the cars (spares not available, cars which would not run for weeks, etc.).

Another common wrong assumption in approaching E.Ms consists in believing that 'these markets are at an earlier stage of the same development path followed by the developed countries (Arnold and Quelch 1998)'. This implies that patterns of evolution followed in these markets will also happen in a similar sequence, in the emerging ones. Once again similar assumptions lead to formulate wrong strategies which will often fail to generate the expected results.

The frequent mistakes in the desk phase are sometimes explained by the scarce availability of reliable

data in the E.M. (see Section 2.2): even the world renowned market research firms fail to provide good
estimates of retail audits in a market where the trade is
extremely fragmented with a very high percentage of
street kiosks as India, or in a market like Russia where
some of the regions might not be accessible for months
due to the weather conditions.

The mistakes happening in the action phase are
mostly consequences of those incurred in the desk
work, whenever the companies do not realize in time
to be heading in the wrong direction and implement
the strategies based on the wrong elements. While we
shall deal more in detail with these kind of mistakes
later, in the chapters dedicated to the working environment and the building of the business model, we can
anticipate that the major ones are those consequent
to lack of cultural sensitivity, wrong time of implementation, wrong elements of the marketing mix, failure to
deal in the appropriate manner with the local institutions, and lack of long-term commitment from the
company.

2.2 First Mover Advantage

In the previous section, we mentioned the timing of
entry among the critical factors which can considerably
influence the results of the launch in an E.M.

Having in mind the forecasts about the BRIC countries, any company which aims for an international expansion to ensure a sustainable growth of its revenues
in the decades to come, should already have a presence,
or at least a business plan ready to enter these countries.
More in general, talking also of E.Ms other than the

BRIC countries, there are factors which would suggest delaying the entry as well as others which would encourage an early move.

We mentioned already the distinctive features of the E.Ms, and recalled that the assessment of their potential may not be particularly easy, also due to the lack of reliable data on the structure of the consumptions and the retail. For as much as a market researcher could try hard to obtain realistic estimate, obstacles such as migrant populations, non-registered outlets and lack of well-structured government statistical data might make his efforts vain. Those who operate in developed countries may take for granted some basic information which are commonly available here, such as the certainty of the date of birth of a person, her residence address, the name of her parents or her fiscal identification number. Much of these data are not available for large parts of the population of E.Ms (birth certificates are often created for ad hoc purposes based on self declaration of the concerned person appearing before a local authority, let alone more structured data such as the fiscal ones; millions of people do not have a home and live in the streets). Some information might on the other hand be available, yet being not at all representative of the population (e.g., the tax paying population could be as low as 2 per cent of the total adult population of the country, as it seems to be the case in India).

On top of this, an E.M. is by definition a country undergoing major changes, where data happens to change drastically in the span of a few years (e.g., the development of modern trade in China: its weight on the total trade varied from 15 per cent to over 40 per cent in less than 10 years; in cities like Shanghai it has already crossed 50 per cent).

Associated with the continuous change and to some extent the cause of it is the political and economic instability characteristic of the E.M., this would result in uncertainty of the legal frames and difficulty of enforcement of the same, as well as frequent changes in the fiscal legislature which could completely invalidate the assumptions of a business plan.[2] Therefore, a company could risk to invest some million dollars in a country with the objective of making profits and repatriate the same to the country of origin; however, some change in fiscal laws (e.g., doubling of excise duty, steep increase of the income taxes) might make its business not profitable; a clause added overnight to an existing law could prevent the company from repatriating the profits gained. Another factor which could discourage from an early entry is the inadequate level of infrastructure, which could mean a higher cost of operating (e.g., the cost of creating a connection with the power grid at one's own expenses, or asphalting and maintaining a road leading to a factory) [see Table 2.1].

TABLE **2.1** STARTING A BUSINESS

Country	Procedures numbers	Duration days	Cost % GNI per capita	Min. capital % GNI per capita
Brazil	17	152	9.9	0.0
Russia	7	28	2.7	3.4
India	11	35	73.7	0.0
China	13	35	9.3	213.1

Source: www.doingbusiness.org/exploretopics/startingbusiness

Note: These data are estimated for the launch of a commercial or industrial firm with up to 50 employees and a start-up capital of 10 times the economy's per capita Gross National Income (GNI); the minimum capital is that prescribed by the law.

However, there are a number of factors which work in the opposite direction, and push the prospective investor to accelerate his entry decision. Most of these are the advantages created by the opportunity of being an early mover in the market, even greater if the move is the first of a category. In this case, the most evident advantage is the benefit of creating a market and succeeding in making the consumers associate the innovative brand with the product category (e.g., Kleenex in the tissues, Cola in the soft drinks, Frigidaire in the refrigerators, etc.). While this is a critical advantage even in a developed market, in an E.M. a number of conditions associated with the early move, create multiplicative effects that could yield unexpected results, particularly when the overall innovation is marketed with the optimal marketing mix. The clear difference in favour of an early mover in an emerging market versus a developed one is the reaction time of the competitors. The presence of a higher number of players who, though not currently competing exactly in the same segment, could in a relative short-term replicate a similar product, makes the time advantage gained in a developed market much shorter than the potential one obtainable in an E.M.

Therefore, the relatively low competition, together with some additional positive circumstances normally experienced in these markets, such as a limited number of advertisers, relatively low cost of advertising and absence of strongly organized trade with high listing fee, may enable the first movers to obtain in a short time a good level of revenues. Thanks to this, the wise entrant will use the resources generated by the incremental sales to increase the competitive spending and create higher entry barrier, thus reducing the risk of upcoming competition and consolidate his market leadership and eventually dominant position.

Additional benefit accruing to the first movers in an E.M. is the opportunity of creating good relationship with the local authorities and institutions, whose presence and interference in the business are usually rather heavy in these markets; this could allow to effectively lobbying in order to obtain special concessions which might not be granted to successive entrants. Some countries, for instance, had decided at a certain point in time, of limiting the number of licenses given to MNCs in many industries (e.g., China during the eighties).

The interaction with the ruling bodies will thus give visibility to the entrant: while this could result in unwanted attention unscrupulous bureaucrats (see Chapter 5, Section 5.1), it would also establish a preferential channel of communication. Through this channel, possible new law projects might be shared in advance with potential investors, and possibly mitigated also in accordance to the suggestions made by the latter.

Sometime an apparent entry barrier could eventually turn into an opportunity to create a unique competitive edge. We mentioned earlier that the lack of infrastructures could hinder the development of sales: this is particularly true in the case of distribution in an E.M., where the absence of well-structured networks and channels might pose serious obstacles to the marketeer who seeks to make his products available among his targeted universe.

Such difficult conditions might leave no option to the entrant but to create his own distribution network, tailor-made for his needs and available resources. While this could initially require an important investment, it might subsequently become a critical success factor as well as an opportunity to generate additional revenues and profits by leveraging on the established network to distribute non-competing products of companies seeking quicker entry in the market.

2.3 Own Forces Vs Partnership

An important dilemma faced by companies wanting to invest in an E.M. is whether to autonomously enter the country by creating a fully owned and independent subsidiary or to set up a joint venture with a local partner.

In some countries (those still relatively less open to foreign direct investment), the choice is not even given since the local laws prescribe that a subsidiary created by a foreign investor has to have local partners in a stated percentage, varying according to the strategic importance of the specific sector for the host country. Within these prescriptions, several socialist countries used to grant approval to foreign investors for ventures in which the local government would hold the majority or at least an important part of the shares. While such norms have been progressively phased out or at least eased off, they are still present for some sectors in many of the E.Ms and particularly in the former communist countries. They represent a true roadblock for those investors who do not like government interference in conducting their business. On the other hand, the norms prescribing compulsory joint venture business with local private partners are easily bypassed through the initial participation of a local financial partner, who does not interfere in managing the venture and gets progressively diluted, according to the evolution of the norms with passing time.

When the option of autonomous entry is legally available (or when ways and means are found to by-pass the existing norms), the solution to the mentioned dilemma must come from the joint evaluation of the objectives of the investing company vis-à-vis the resources budgeted for the project and the working environment of the country considered.

A company that would desire to gain rapid access to the country culture, business network and institutional relationship might decide to go for a partnership with a local player who could provide all this. In this case, an accurate choice of the local partner becomes extremely important in order to avoid unpleasant surprises.

The first screening of a possible partnership should analyse the compatibility of the values and cultures of the two companies. It is advisable to go in-depth in this study, since the dominant values of an organization are often better found in the day-to-day practices experienced in the market as well as in the informal organizational structure, other than in the mission/value statements and the corporate brochures. A well worth exercise to get a clear picture of a prospect local partner consists of informal and anonymous discussion with its vendors, clients and employees. In some countries the selection of a partner requires a detailed analysis which may last some months. In China, for instance, local partners may have strong political connections with relevant authorities, who may actually be the main stakeholders in the venture-to-be, whereas the negotiating entity is only the frontline representative for them. Foreign investors may be eager to finalize an agreement in a short time, but, by doing this, they risk to eventually accept sub-optimal compromises in order to end the frustration of a distressing negotiation.

Sometimes the choice of the foreign investor falls on local partners operating in the same industry, in order to leverage on their know-how. This decision could appear as a quick win but it often leads to potential problems, since the local partner would then tend to follow his established way of operating rather than adopting the one wanted by the investor, thus leading to clashes. Alternatively, the local partner could, once he has absorbed the international know-how from the foreign associates, decide to break the venture and apply the acquired knowledge in an own set-up. Many such examples are available within the international case histories (Piaggio and Bajaj in India, Unilever and White Cat in China); despite these, many investors continue to repeat the same mistake. Rather than an important player in the same industry, a better choice could be a relatively less established and entrepreneurial player in a similar industry, who could prove definitely more change-oriented as well as potentially less dangerous. It is anyway strongly recommended that the investor maintains the majority of the shares, so as to be able to retain the possibility of having the last word in the strategic choices.

The frequent matter of disagreement between foreign investors and local partners apart from the above-mentioned ones are the different expectations: the former tend to build the business with a longer term perspective, whereas the latter are often more interested in short-term results and particularly in profits. This would normally lead to contrasts in strategic choices concerning investments and organizational choices.

When such clashes become more and more frequent up to the level of creating roadblocks to the running of the business, the partnership ends, sometimes with a mutual agreement that normally leads to the dilution and eventual take-over of the local partners' shares by the foreign investor; at other times, a consensus is not found and the case ends up in the law court, with consequent waste of time and resources by both partners. Such contrasts also divert the management attention from the business, thus aggravating the negative impact on the same.

An exhaustive examination of the joint ventures in E.Ms would probably reveal that many of them would be problematic (Prahalad and Lieberthal 1998): this has led to a progressively lower number of them since the learning of the negative experience has been applied in more countries. An example of this is found in a survey conducted in China: here the government began to allow 100 per cent foreign-owned ventures in 1986, though there had been special cases on exception basis earlier.[3] After merely six years from this opening the wholly owned enterprises already represented 18 per cent of the Direct Foreign Investment; four years later, in 1986, this percentage had grown to become 37 per cent (ibid).

Notes

1. A typical example of this in the FMCG Sector is the consumption of bubble gums: these products are almost exclusively consumed by children in Western markets and equally chewed by adults, teenagers and children in a market like India. Another example in consumer durables comes from the launch of Ford Escort, conceived in India as middle-class car but priced at a level which in this country only niche consumers

could afford; the same consumers would rather buy a bigger car and more expensive one.

2. In Bangladesh, custom duty for goods imported from India increased from 20 per cent to 100 per cent between 1999 to 2002. This has happened despite a stated commitment to reduce and eventually remove duties within the SAARC countries, the cooperation among South Asian countries of which both India and Bangladesh are active members.

3. In March 1983, 3M became the first wholly-owned foreign enterprise in China.

References

Arnold, D.J. and J. Quelch. 1998. 'New Strategies in Emerging Markets', *Harvard Business Review*.

Cavusgil, S.T., P. Ghauri and M. Agarwal. 2002. *Doing Business in Emerging Markets*, New Delhi: Sage Publications.

Prahalad, C.K. and K. Lieberthal. 1998. 'The End of Corporate Imperialism', *Harvard Business Review*.

3

WORKING ENVIRONMENT

The strong take from the weak, but the smart take from the strong —Anonymous

3.1 Internal Resources

Informed decision-making comes from a long tradition of guessing and then blaming others for inadequate results —S. Adams

3.1.1 Expatriates

Once the decision of entering an E.M. is made, the investor will need to start implementing the strategies retained in the business plan and make the first steps in actually building the business model to operate.

In order to do so he will have to thoroughly analyse the practical aspects of the working environment, so as to make the right choices that will eventually determine the success of his venture. He will therefore appoint a managerial resource who will be in charge of structuring the new organization and running it as per the guidelines received. The choice of this resource is a very important one since it will influence most of the decisions to be subsequently taken; it needs therefore careful pondering. If the investor is a Multinational Company (MNC), the choice would normally fall on an expatriate, and possibly someone who has been in the company already for some time, thus he is aligned with the culture and values of the same and has the trust of the shareholders. Expatriates are also selected in the initial stage of the operation in order to transfer technology and management policies to the local resources, as well as to ensure a consistent flow of information between the developing unit and the headquarter.

While selecting the expatriate who will be in charge of the E.C., the company will have to take extra care to ensure that the right resource is hired. He/she will need an adequate dose of adaptability to the local conditions, the capability of understanding the local culture and habits as well as the commitment to implement the corporate guidelines within the local context.

A person who has spent most of his career in the 'protected environment' of the corporate office of a well-structured organization in a developed country, might not be the ideal person to be sent to set up a green field project in West Africa. Similarly, the work experience of the selected person should be in line with the retained mission of the local venture. Some MNCs have the internal practice of appointing as Country Manager, a resource with sales and marketing background and experience; such a choice would not be the ideal in case the set-up to be developed is to be mainly a manufacturing or a processing unit, with no interest in selling to the local market; an engineer with experience in production and logistics would clearly be a more effective resource for such a context (see Figure 3.1).

FIGURE 3.1 DIFFERENT PROFILES OF EXPATRIATES AT DIFFERENT STAGES OF MARKET ACTIVITIES

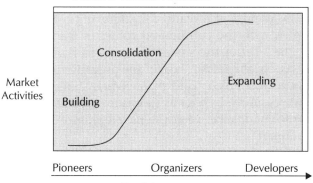

Profile of the Expatriate

Source: Lasserre and Schutte, 1995.

Last, but not the least, the personal situation of the candidate should be an important element for the decision: a recently married manager with a few-months-old child and an expecting wife would certainly not be an ideal candidate for a posting in an E.C. where sanitary structures are not always ideal. As a more general suggestion, it would be advisable to select candidates with a stable family situation (e.g., single or married with grown-up children) to ensure that possible family related problems do not have a defocusing influence on his performances, or on his willingness to remain in the position for the agreed duration of the posting.[1]

Proof of this is found in a recent survey (Hill 2001) on American expatriates sent to developing countries, which show that two out of the five reasons of failure of international posting are related to family problems (see Box 3.1).

BOX 3.1 REASONS FOR THE FAILURE OF EXPATRIATE POSTINGS

a) Inability of the spouse to adjust
b) Inability of the manager to adjust
c) Other family problems
d) Manager's personal or emotional maturity
e) Inability to cope with larger overseas responsibilities

Source: Cavusgil et al., (2002).

A recommended time threshold for significant contribution of a senior manager in an E.C. would be three years. The reason behind this is that the first year would be necessary for him to learn about the country, the working environment and the local practices; the second would see him starting to contribute and still learn out of his direct experience; the third would allow him to fully impact the business thanks to the acquired knowledge, also because by that time he is likely to have a settled personal life.

While some MNCs do follow such minimum duration practice, some others (e.g., B.A.T.) prefer to shorten the period to 18–30 months, so as to give the opportunity to the resources to gain exposure in different countries through horizontal movements in similar positions across them.

Different companies have different approaches towards the deployment of expatriates: some prefer to have a larger number of international resources in most of the functions, so as to make sure that all corporate guidelines are followed across the departments and a fully transparent flow of communication with the headquarter is ensured. Usually these companies would have a large pool of expatriates moving across the international subsidiaries, as well as some in the headquarter, for periods of corporate training and exposure; they would come not only from the country of origin of the company but also from the sister companies, affiliates and worldwide subsidiaries.

In these cases, the expatriates usually have local contracts, thus do not maintain a dual relation with the country of origin and with the one where they are posted, but they are only employees of the latter. They form part of a group that has chosen to pursue an international career; they will keep on moving throughout locations, without a commitment from the company to ensure their repatriation. These resources would normally have faster careers and relatively more remunerative packages as a premium to be paid to them for their continuous mobility.[2]

Other companies have a completely different approach: they would deploy a limited number of expatriates manning only the top management key positions (GM, CFO, Head of Process/Quality, etc.). They would possibly reduce the number of international resources down to one or two once the company has stabilized its operations in a certain country. In such cases the expatriates would mainly be coming from the country of origin of the company, and would maintain an international contract with a double employment relationship with the local subsidiary as well as with the headquarter.

The remuneration of expatriates is a crucial element to ensure the stability of the resources: often in E.Cs it might happen to lose experts who have acquired a good knowledge of the local market and get hired by other foreign companies at much higher packages. The overall compensation should be such to ensure a very comfortable quality of life to the family while not being disproportionately higher than that earned by a local resource in the same position.

In general, there is no ideal policy to be universally utilized, but particularly for E.Cs it is advisable to have a balanced blend of international knowledge and local competence. In the start-up phase a larger number of expatriates could be useful to ensure an adequate training and the implementation of corporate strategies. At a later stage, if there are potential local resources that prove to be able to take over and handle the business, it is recommended to scale down the number of expatriates. However, particularly for E.Cs where the local practices might be subject to pressure from a corrupted external environment, it is advisable that strict systems of corporate governance be put in place and a minimal presence of international resources either in the top management or in the Board of Directors be maintained. This would also help the local subsidiary's credibility and 'share of voice' (Prahalad and Lieberthal 1998) at the corporate headquarter, while ensuring that the ordinary running of the company is effected by local resources, with a 'much better appreciation of local nuances and a deeper commitment to the local market than any expatriate could have' (ibid).

As a thumb rule, the net salary perceived by the expatriate, without considering the housing and the children education, should be comparable to that of a local resource, when the relocation and hardship allowances are not considered.

While the relocation allowance is normally granted to all expatriates and is often a percentage of the basic salary (say 15 or 20 per cent), the hardship one faces depends on the actual difficulties and discomfort that the resource and family might encounter in the country of posting. This therefore, might also not be paid when the movement happens in countries considered more comfortable places to live than the one of origin (e.g., a Mexican family moving to the USA). However, even when the hardship allowance is not paid, an index of cost of living is considered, so as to ensure an adequate purchasing power to the expatriate relocated.

Apart from the compensation, the other key factors to keep expatriates motivated are certainly the challenge of the job (this would even come before the salary package in survey (Conway 1994), the professional and personal development and the long-term career. One more factor which is highly valued by entrepreneurial expatriates is the relatively high degree of autonomy they would enjoy in such postings vis-à-vis a more limited role they might have played at the headquarters. For different personalities such autonomy could on the other hand be perceived as an insufficient support from the central supporting departments. However, the main concerns from the expatriate's point of view would be the possible re-integration at the moment of coming back, as well as the fear of being forgotten, often associated to an unclear length of the posting. Companies who want to retain their international resources should attend to these concerns through exhaustive letters of appointment including clear conditions of expatriation and pre-defined career paths, which could give at least a tentative idea of the future postings, if certain con-ditions are present and if the agreed objectives are achieved.

3.1.2 Local Talent

Irrespective of the expatriate policy of the mother company, most of the resources of the local organization would be people of local origin. They will therefore, play a major role in ensuring the success of the venture in the country. It is a fact that organizations are done by people, and no company can succeed without the support of the right resources.

In the E.Cs the selection of talented people might not be an easy matter and the help of a reliable consultant could prove to be very useful. If the scale of recruitment foreseen for the local organization is rather large, it would be advisable to hire at an early stage a local H.R. Manager: his knowledge of the available human capital, their strengths and weaknesses and the potential downsides will certainly help reduce the risks of wrong recruitments and the negative consequences of the same.

The abundance of high potential resources varies according to different countries: some of these are known to have very good task executors and high manual capability people, thus excellent candidates for shop floor activities such as manufacturing and processing. This is the case in the East Asia countries, such as China, Korea and Taiwan. Other countries are better known to have a larger availability of technical know-how, thus being a good source for engineers or other technical or managerial resources: Japan and to some extent Russia are amongst these. Other E.Cs such as India have abundant resources with an interesting mixture of high technical skills, such as Information Technology, as well as a fair amount of creativity and people orientation. This explains why a higher and higher number of IT engineers move every year directly from the Indian post-graduation institutes to large American software firms and also why many major IT design companies are creating in India their global production centres.[3] It also explains why a growing number of multinational companies decide to utilize India as a base for the production of international advertising commercials, which are shot here at a fraction of the cost one would incur in Europe or USA, while being recognized among the most creative in international advertising awards circuits.[4]

Many of the E.Cs were colonies of European countries at some moment in their history: this has left traces still present in the attitude of the local resources in their interaction with expatriates. Often this translates in a form of higher respect towards 'the white man'; some other time the sentiment is not fully positive, and international resources might be looked at with distrust, sometimes with envy or even with unnecessary competitiveness, as those who may prevent the growth of talented local resources. It is therefore, advisable to place the expatriates and the indigenous executives on equal footing, so as to minimize possible difficulties in the relationship as well as unnecessary discrimination: expatriates will clearly have the normal perquisites and compensation in line with the international HR Policy, but they should not be treated as privileged members of the team, if a good level of motivation among the internal resources is to be maintained.

While grooming local recruits in E.Cs one has to consider that the influence of the personal life on the work performances is usually larger than what one would experience in developed countries. In many cases, the salary of the local worker will be the only source of income of a large family, with many people depending on him; in some countries the concept of extended family is still quite common, thus the decisions of the employee might be heavily influenced by some of the members of the same and not be left to the individual only; frequent requests of leaves to attend celebrations of relatively distant relatives (sister's mother-in-law's cousins) could sound quite unusual and unjustified in the eyes of an European Manager: however, the denial of the same might even cause the resignation of the individual.

Also for these reasons, the position of the Chief HR is extremely important in such contexts, since he helps those responsible for business to perceive the nuances of the local psychology and act accordingly. This position might become very powerful within the company, since those who eventually are hired in the organization often feel personally indebted and look at him with a mixture of thankfulness and fear which make him a quasi-god. Such kind of relationships are clearly better avoided, in order to ensure that all management team members have a balanced role in the company and no specific head of department overpowers the other and acquires a disproportionate importance in the eyes of the employees.

The Chief Executive Officers (CEOs) of companies operating in E.Cs will have to adjust their style of management to the local culture in order to maximize their effectiveness. They will need to be much more directive in countries like China where managers look forward to receiving written guidelines and formulae to follow: they should use a more flexible and delegating approach with Indian managers, who are used to be given more independence and responsibility; they will need a firm and directive but respectful attitude in Russia, where executives might seem detached but have immense pride and sometimes temperamental behaviours.

At the same time, CEOs will have to be ready to devote an important share of their time to sort out conflicts among their managers: as a matter of fact, it is quite frequent that those who have made it to the level of senior managers, and had to fight hard to achieve this position, will continue to struggle to ensure their moving up in the organizational ladder, even at the expense of their colleagues. This implies that, with the objective of gaining mileage in the eyes of their boss, they will not hesitate to point out their peers' faults, sometimes real mistakes, sometimes rather 'interpreted' by them so as to show 'how some issue could have been dealt with in a much better way'.

Sometimes this is the result of a competitive attitude they have acquired during their years of education or their professional career; other times a similar attitude derives from the culture of the country where they have been living. For instance 'the Chinese do not separate the personal and professional, so power struggles and politics often dominate Chinese corporate behaviour' (Mc Gregor 2005). In the case of China (see Box 3.2), there is also an accentuated distrust for the system which drives a distrust in '...everyone outside one's immediate family or circle of close friends. This has created a business environment that is steeped in dishonesty and in dire need of transparency and fair dispute resolution systems' (Mc Gregor 2005).

Box 3.2 Interpersonal Relationships in China

The principle of *pao* is a concept proper to the Chinese culture that provides the explanation of the flexibility in managing the interpersonal relationship often found in Chinese resources. Literally the word means one's honor to another, but widely speaking it could be translated as doing favors. These are considered as a form of social investment for which some kind of return is expected. The concept is applicable to the family life (Parents fostering children who are expected to repay the parental care) as it is to the business circumstances. The concept is in someway related to another very important one which is the *guanxi* (literally connections), which pushes the businessmen to closely cultivate some important relationships. These concepts are the basis of the big global Chinese networks, and explain the strength and the flourishing of the Chinese communities in Western countries.

Source: Capon and Vanhonacker 1999.

India would be different in this: while even in this case it is known that the system is bureaucratic and often corrupt, however, there is still a certain sense of trust in some of the institutional authorities, particularly at high levels (e.g., the respect and esteem that the business community has for the highest level of the Indian judiciary system, the High Courts and the Supreme Court of Justice, is easily perceivable). However, centuries of caste system have created a kind of natural segmentation among business groups, thanks to which those who belong to a caste would trust much more and therefore tend to associate to business people of the same caste. In a more general perspective, even within an organization, there could be a behaviour which is biased towards the members of the same community or caste.

In Russia, such a bias could derive from the region of origin of the people; therefore, in Moscow, people coming from St. Petersburg could have a slight disadvantage versus those of Moscow origin, which could be even more accentuated in case of other ethnic groups coming, for instance, from the former Soviet Republics. Incidentally, Russians show sometime also in the workplace a certain 'racist' attitude, particularly towards people coming from countries that are sometimes considered as 'inferior' in their eyes: this can be an important decision element while considering the possibility of posting in Russia an expatriate of origin from one of those countries (see Box 3.3).

Box 3.3 Hiring and Developing Local Talent

The majority of 3M employees in Asia come from the countries in which they work. The rational behind this is their better knowledge of their customers, suppliers, local laws and culture vis-à-vis some possible expatriates: also, they can speak the local language, therefore, communicate better with local people. Other international companies such as McDonnel Douglas have a similar approach, and hire more and more local resources for their operation in Asia: this is the case, for instance, in China, where a larger number of Chinese or Chinese speaking Americans are hired to take care of their mainland business. The expatriates in the region are however trained in the local language.

Source: Kotler et al. 1999.

3.1.3 Cultural Intelligence (C.I.)

Every society has values, habits, beliefs and communication tools that ensure the interaction of its members and govern the social life of the same: in brief, every community has its own culture.

When a new member joins a community, he is progressively inducted in its culture through a process that makes him experience and understand the elements of it. In tribal societies, the process goes through several rites and the candidate can only be considered a full-fledged member after he has successfully completed some crucial steps which prove that he has been able to absorb the necessary knowledge and skills to be part of the tribe. Similar rituals are still present in modern societies, even if they are not any more considered as mystic rituals but rather as normal stages of the social life: a graduation ceremony, an engagement one or the prize distribution after a sports event are examples of this.

In the professional life of a manager, joining a new company represents a process that is to some extent equivalent to becoming a member of a tribe. During the induction period, the joinee will have to listen, communicate with the colleagues, learn the company policies and understand both the formal and the informal sides of the organization, so as to be able to effectively work in it and represent it towards the external partners. Depending on the complexity of the industry where the company operates as well as the size of the same and the number of years of operation, the process could take from a few weeks to a few years to be completed:

actually speaking it could never be considered as completed since organizations are continuously changing. Also, within a sizeable organization several sub-cultures are likely to co-exist: therefore, the production personnel would not necessarily fully understand the logic of marketing people, and the legal department officers might not really get along and empathize with the sales crowd, and so on.

A person who has the ability to rapidly perceive the key elements of a certain organization, family or society and adapt his behaviour so as to have a better interaction with their members can be defined as having a high Cultural Intelligence (C.I.). Such a capability is often a natural gift in people who have since their childhood developed it thanks to circumstances that have exposed them to very different environments: this could be the case for the children of a family who have lived in several countries due to the job of one of the parents. Such individuals, who have had to stay in different countries, learn different languages and live in very different environments, are likely to develop a higher sensitivity and flexibility compared to others who have always lived in one place, have been exposed to one society and have grown up with a close number of people in a relatively stable and stagnant culture.

From an organizational point of view, the concept of C.I. has some element of the Emotional Intelligence (E.I.) theorized by Goleman (1995). People with high E.I. quotient are able to perceive non-rational or logical sides of human behaviours and empathize with people they interact with. Those with a high level of C.I. would go a step further: having understood the cultural roots of a certain behaviour, they would be able to absorb part of it and adapt their own behaviour to the one

considered, so as to appear to their counterpart as talking the same language and sharing a similar culture.
Therefore, C.I. is certainly a very important skill to
effectively do business in a developing country.

A recent article (Earley and Rosakowath 2004) defines
C.I. as 'an outsider's seemingly natural ability to inter-
pret someone's unfamiliar and ambiguous gestures the
way that person's compatriots would'.

We can notice that this definition poses the accent
on the natural ability and on the geographical differentiation between gestures peculiar to some countries and
not to the others. While we also mentioned that such
skill is often a natural gift, we are also convinced that
it can be developed with time and practice. We also
believe that other elements apart from the geographical
one can make cultures extremely different, whereas
within the same country there could be very dissimilar
habits and values. An example of this could be found
in India, where the behaviour and culture of people of
northern and southern states are different; on the other
hand many elements of South Indian society are found
not only in countries such as Sri Lanka, Maldives,
Mauritius, but also in Singapore and Thailand.

More, in general, we could say that the ability to
understand the social behaviour and the value orientation of a group with a given culture, be this group a
country, a region, or an ethnic cluster, and adopt some
elements of these in one's interpersonal approaches,
clearly increases the chances of successful results while
doing business in E.Ms (see Box 3.4).

In order to be more specific, let us consider the South
East Asia group of countries, and try to draw an East–
West macro comparison, so as to highlight some of the
main elements that a Western European individual will

Box 3.4 NEGOTIATIONS IN BRAZIL

Brazilians value highly loyalty and trust: building personal relationship in such a culture is therefore very important, and it could carry more weight than an impressive presentation. Negotiations risk then to be influenced by subjective feelings; often they focus on achieving short-term results. Being flexible is certainly a common characteristic of the Brazilian people: while confronted with difficult problems they act with 'jeito', that means to find a way around things. Conflict and confrontation are not part of their temperament. Also, remember to go to the highest level of the hierarchy for a quicker finalization: decisions are taken at the highest rank in their business culture. When the meeting is over, do not rush off: Brazilians may take that as a personal insult.

Source: 'HSBC, Business Connections, Your Guide to Business Culture Around the World', insert in *Time* 2002.

have to analyse and factor in his effort to become a culturally intelligent actor.

One of the immediate differences he will perceive in the social behaviour of this region is the strong social pressure to comply with group norms which is spread across Asia. While the last decades of the twentieth century have seen in Western countries the loud statement of the social rights of being different, and diversity has progressively become not only tolerated but sometimes sanctioned by law or even trendy,[5] being different for Asians, feel uncomfortable. This is partly explained by the influence of Confucianism, still rooted in many Asian societies, which 'plays a central role in orchestrating interpersonal relationships' (Capon and Vanhonacker 1999). Some of the principles of this require that an individual strives to achieve social harmony through a behaviour which ensures his social accept-ability. Therefore, while 'Westerns assume that indi-viduals act in their own self interest, make decisions rationally and are in control of their destiny... Asians perceive one's existence in society as largely influenced by relationships with others that one cannot change; rather, one must harmonize with the environment' (Capon and Vanhonacker 1999).

Such social rules are also in some way in line with the concept of extended family quoted earlier in this chapter, still present in many Asian societies, which implies that the group goals have the primacy over the individual ones.

Another easily perceivable difference between the West and the East, which is again partly explained by the religious background, is the concept of fate and destiny, spread not only in the South East Asian region but also in the Indian subcontinent. Here it is believed that life is a combination of human acts as well as pre-determined circumstances, where the weight of these circumstances is rather large. Thus, not much can be done to change one's destiny. Also in this case, the atti-tude of Western people is definitely less resigned and more willing to fight the events to affirm their will.

Another extremely important element to be always kept in mind while dealing with Asians is the concept of 'face'. In many of the Asian societies the loss of face is so important as to prevent the individual from lead-ing a normal life and sometimes bringing the same to the extreme consequence of suicide. While this concept plays a major role particularly in the Chinese cultures,[6] where its loss makes community life impossible, it is also present in Japan, in Thailand and in South Asia. The 'saving of the face' has large implications in the work behaviour and is one of the frequent matters of problems between expatriates and local resources.

All these concepts, including the attempt to avoid direct conflict, are more or less related and contribute to create a high degree of interpersonal sensitivity in the Asian culture. A Western individual with low C.I. might not fully perceive these aspects, or might take a long time to understand them, and consequently might behave in such ways to be considered not acceptable both professionally and socially. On the other hand, a person with a developed cultural sensitivity will be able to absorb the important elements of the local social rules and have a smooth interaction with the different societies, thus achieving better integration and performance.

3.2 External Forces

The incestuous relationship between government and big business thrives in the dark —Jack Anderson

3.2.1 Institutions

A company operating in a foreign country will necessarily need to keep interacting with the political and administrative machine of the same. In an E.M. the role of the government in the economic and social scenario is usually more prominent than in a developed one, thus its interference in the business is rather frequent (see Figure 3.2). Learning how to manage at the best the interaction with the local institutions is therefore a matter of capital importance.

FIGURE 3.2 GOVERNMENT INFLUENCE IN BUSINESS AS PERCEIVED
BY WESTERN MANAGERS

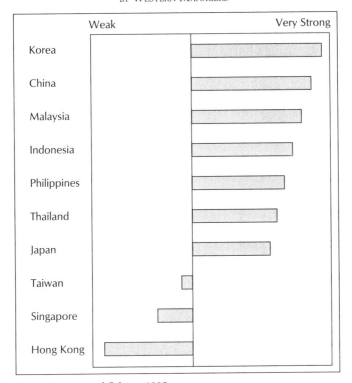

Source: Lasserre and Schutte 1995.

The local management will need to understand their mechanism of functioning, the dominant culture, the hierarchy and importance of the officers, in order to acquire the appropriate skills to successfully deal with bureaucrats and politicians. It will also be useful to realize that the institutions will often have objectives different from the ones of the company. Local employment, tax income, foreign reserves, balance of payment and many other similar points will be priority matters in the agenda of the former and might not be fully in line with the business plan of the latter.

It will rarely happen that the company will succeed in obtaining all that it had planned and a long process of negotiation with concessions from both the parties will eventually lead to a compromise which has mutual benefits (see Figure 3.3).

FIGURE 3.3 STRATEGIC APPROACHES TO GOVERNMENT RELATIONS

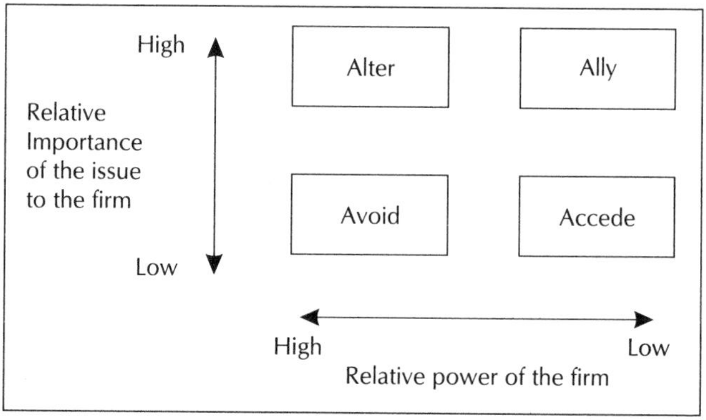

Source: Cavusgil et al. 2002.

The use of local consultants can be very helpful in these circumstances: international firms with local resources will combine the reputation of the international brand name with the knowledge and experience of people well familiar with the functioning of the rules and regulations of the country.

While some E.M. institutions have adopted an open and progressive attitude towards foreign investors and have set the example by starting to include in the public sector the principles of modern business management, some others have not yet followed the same route. The most progressive countries (e.g., Singapore, South Korea) are those that have promoted a well-educated and business-oriented bureaucracy, which understands the needs of corporations. This allows them to consider with a different perspective the requests of the companies. Also, thanks to this new generation of civil servants, the public sector makes the first steps towards a functioning model similar to the private one.

In some E.Cs the government intervenes directly in the business through the ownership and control of part of the enterprises (e.g., China, Vietnam). However, over time, direct ownership of private ventures has been decreasing (see Box 3.5) and some countries have also started an intentional privatization drive, e.g., Malaysia, Philippines (Lasserre and Schutte 1995).

Box 3.5 Exxon and Yukos in Russia

In 2003 strong rumors about Exxon taking an important share (40 to 50 per cent) in Yukos, a major Russian oil company, appeared in the press. Rumors talked also of a possible takeover in the main management positions of the company by a group of American managers, who would be hired by the main shareholder, M. Khordokovsky, to change the management style and improve the performance of the company. The government realized what was happening and showed an ambiguous attitude towards the facts, initially appearing favorable, but eventually resulting in opposition, given the strategic importance of the sector. Rumors say that the opportunity to avoid an 'Americanization' of Russian strategic sectors, together with the growing popularity of Khordokovsky, who had been mainly responsible for these developments in the venture and was also seen as a possible future candidate to the Kremlin in

(Box 3.5—continued)

(*Box 3.5—continued*)

the upcoming elections, caused the Government's reaction during 2005 in the matter (including the criminal procedures against the Chairman, still in prison at the moment when we write). Exxon had little choice but reducing their exposure in the venture. The Yukos CEO (S. Theede) went to self-imposed exile in London after the media reported that he did not have a valid work permit.

Establishing a good equation with the local authorities is the suggested route to ensure a smooth business. While not always is it possible to do so, and sometimes it might be necessary to adopt a confrontation approach, the company must be aware that while doing this, there are chances that the operations in that country might come to a temporary or sometimes permanent halt. Something on this line happened to Coca-Cola in India. The company had been present for some years in the market (Hindustan Cola) when in 1977 requests from the government tried to impose a revelation of the Coca-Cola formulation. Rather than abiding to such a request, the company chose to leave the country to come back only after 15 years.

When negotiating with government officers, it is advisable to try and reach the highest level of the hierarchy, since at that position the probability of discussing with a reasonable and understanding counterpart are certainly higher. Also, at lower levels the corruption is much more spread and despite comprehending the good intentions of the private investors, the bureaucrats might try to create hurdles so as to take personal advantage of the situation. One way to maintain good relationship with government officers is to regularly go and visit them, also when a meeting is not necessarily needed: since companies and individuals would seek to meet them when some intervention from them is required, a courtesy visit would certainly contribute to build a favourable impression on which one could bank in more difficult situations.

Business legislation has several purposes: the main ones are to protect the interest of the society from unscrupulous business behaviour; to protect consumers from unfair business practices; and also to protect companies from unfair competition (Kotler et al. 1999). While the first of these would normally be quite prominent in E.Ms, the other two are not often effectively implemented in these markets. In fact, the protection ensured to consumers by the enforcing authorities and by the consumers' associations is rather limited, since these associations do not carry the weight of those of the developed countries. The last chance left to those who have been in some way damaged is to appeal to the courts of justice, which are not always particularly efficient, hence, the risk of waiting for years to obtain a judgment, the effect of which, in most cases, from a mere economic perspective do not even compensate the legal expenses incurred.

Similarly, also the companies' protection laws would often be ineffective. Cases of legislations passed to protect home industries would not be rare in these countries, whereas trademarks and patent protection and more in general, intellectual property are often left to the capability of the international company of finding a way to enforce the laws. At times this will be done by convincing the local police to cooperate in seizing the stock of the copy-cat found in the market and close the factory producing the same, measures which have only temporary and limited effects.

Institutions in Africa

Box 3.6 FACILITATING INVESTMENTS IN AFRICA

The Investment Climate Facility for Africa is a public–private partnership, funded by companies, bilateral and multilateral donors, and is expected to become fully operational in mid-2006 once donors and companies make their commitments. It aims to raise USD 550 million during its seven year lifespan. Once it is established, the funds will go towards lowering the cost of doing business in Africa in order to improve the investment climate and allow African entrepreneurship to flourish. So far, the UK has announced that it will commit USD 30 million to the project, and Anglo American, Royal Dutch Shell and the Shell Foundation have also announced that they will each commit USD 2.5 million.

The ICF will be established as an independent trust and will be governed by a board of trustees, mostly Africans. It will allow countries to adopt more business-friendly policies, laws and regulations across the continent and strengthen the institutions that will enforce these laws. Furthermore, most African countries have high barriers of entry and the costs of private sector capital are not low enough for the factors of production to have the required mobility needed to withstand external shocks. Consequently, the ICF will help to support projects such as streamlining business registrations and licensing systems, reforming customs administration and taxation, and removing barriers to competition. It will also build on earlier success stories such as a successful pilot program in Entebbe, Uganda, which shortened the new business registration time from two days to just 30 minutes; and a custom reform program in Mozambique that allows goods to be cleared up to 40 times faster than previously.

Source: Dun & Bradstreet on 'India in Perspective', February 2006.

BOX 3.7 SOMALIA PHONES

Somalia, a country without a government since 1991, despite its difficult economic and political situation, has witnessed an unlikely success story in telecoms. Possibly thanks to the lack of regulation a call from a Somali mobile phone is generally cheaper and clearer than a call from anywhere else in Africa. Private mobile companies moved in and found that the collapsed state provided a curious competitive advantage.

Because of the absence of government the telecom company did not need to worry about corrupt ministry officials to pay off, and could freely choose the best value equipment. Taxes and security deposit are approximately 5% and customs duties are very low. Also, there is no need to pay for licenses, or to pay to put up masts.

Golis Telecom, one of the larger forces in the Somali market, foresees to have 50,000 mobile subscribers by 2007. Their investment was as low as USD 2.7million for Chinese equipment purchased to set up its service. The cost of an international call is very low, at USD 0.30 a minute, but the low cost of the set-up makes the business still viable.

The lack of government turns out to be a definite advantage in this case.

BOX 3.8 SUDDEN CHANGE OF LAWS IN AFRICA

A renowned MNC operating in an African country used to procure from Europe an ingredient for one of their products. At a certain point in time and without a previous notice, the import of this ingredient was declared banned. Unfortunately at that moment, a container with the same was already sailing: when it reached the port of the country, the custom authorities

(*Box 3.8—continued*)

(*Box 3.8—continued*)

> stopped it and kept it in their bonded warehouse. The Company tried to explain that the container had been sent when the ingredient was still legally importable in the country, but, despite long and articulated procedures, did not succeed in clearing the container. The local CEO of the Company had to personally intervene and meet the highest custom in charge, and thanks to this, after almost one year, the goods moved to the next level, the port authorities. However, in the meantime, the case had become quite known within the concerned people, and the officers here thought that, to sort out the situation at the previous level, some large amount of money had been paid and thus expected to receive similar treatment. The reality was that the sorting of the matter had taken that long because the Company had not wanted to pay easy money. The whole process took eventually some more time to be resolved and since the arrival of the goods, more than one year had passed by the time the product could be brought to the Company's premises.

3.2.2 Suppliers

The analysis of the availability of materials is one of the factors considered in the preliminary feasibility study leading to the decision of investment in a certain country.

Generally speaking, an E.M. will have a more restricted base of suppliers vis-à-vis a developed one.[7] This will imply a more limited choice among them, which might lead to higher prices.

It is known that the power of suppliers increases in situations of scarcity of the same, particularly when their concentration is higher than the industry to which they sell (Porter 1980). Varying with the sector of activity considered but again generally speaking, the number of possible substitutes to the goods or services supplied would typically be lower in the E.Cs,[8] and this would again contribute to create a position of strong suppliers' power. When decision of entry in a certain country was driven mainly by the availability of materials or talent (see Chapter 1, Section 1.3), the supplied material is a vital item for the buyer's business; also in those circumstances, the suppliers[9] end up having a key role.

All those cases show common situations in E.Cs where buyers (foreign/local corporations) have a relatively low purchasing power and their business might be highly dependent on (few) key suppliers. Such cases partly explain why costs of materials are not always relatively low and competitive with the corresponding ones in developed countries.

There are however, ways also in E.Cs to obtain the best possible conditions with the local suppliers. The precondition of this is to consider the relationship between vendor–buyer as a long-term partnership, which needs to yield mutual benefits. Everywhere in the business world a company will improve its results by building a good rapport with its suppliers: however in E.C. often relationships drive business. A few suggestions will be helpful in developing a sound partnership with those vendors which will have been identified as strategic ones after a structured qualification process.

A continuous communication flow and a limited sharing of company's objectives with them will help make them feel involved and important for the success of the same. The 'stick and carrot' technique is very effective while dealing with them: firm negotiations to obtain the best possible prices, but helping hands in case of terms of payments, or acceptance of quantities in excess of those stated in the order, could be examples of this.

In E.M. it is not rare to receive requests for advances, since particularly small-medium suppliers might not have the necessary funds to procure big quantities of raw materials to process, or to invest in the machineries necessary to produce the output to be supplied. While such requests for facilitations should happen only in special circumstances, the help given in case of necessity will often be a good platform on which one could build to gain the extra discount needed to obtain the budgeted prices.

It might also be necessary to develop brand new vendors since the required material is currently not available in the local market, or it is available but at a high price, as there is only one source of the same, which is banking on its monopoly to command a premium. In these cases, the buying company will have to work closely with the supplier to be developed, in order to give him all the necessary inputs to upgrade its current production or to start a new one. The process might require time and the deployment of resources from the buying company, however, in the majority of cases its payback is well worth the initial effort, and the new vendor will probably become a long-term associate to count upon. The risk in this case is that once the supplier has been brought up to a good level of quality, he might propose his services to some competitor, who would enjoy the results of the upgraded supply. This may be avoided with a contract of exclusivity which could bind the developed supplier (for the newly developed item) to the company for the first 12 to 24 months. Such agreements are common when new technologies are developed in partnership between the buyers and vendors. Here in general, it is extremely important to be perceived as a fair and stable customer to the eyes of the vendor. A growing business with the prospect to buy more in future and reliable and punctual payments are key assets for a supplier. A company that can capitalize on these factors in the E.C. should normally be able to obtain prices below the market average, as well as run smoothly its operations without business interruptions due to supply issues.

3.2.3 Competitors

The level of competition that a company will face in an E.M. will depend on the time of its entry as well as on the development stage of the market in which it will operate.

As mentioned in Chapter 2, Section 2.2, an early entry in a relatively developed industry could give the benefits of the first mover, among which is a lower level of competition. However, even in this case, the entrant would normally have to face the reaction of the local players. These might have started creating hurdles already from an earlier stage, by lobbying with the local authorities in order to keep the market closed to foreign investors so as to protect the home industry.

Local competitors may operate on the whole country/ territory or be present only in regions. They would usually have their stronghold in the territories surrounding their production facilities, where their distribution will be very good and they will also enjoy the support of the municipalities and local politicians, with whom they might have some job-in-exchange-of-favours relationship. In case of countries structured as federal republics, they would have managed to obtain some fiscal incentives (tax waivers, etc.) which could also derive from the fact of having their manufacturing set-up in a certain region or state, when the national organization of the indirect taxation is such to foresee entry taxes for goods not produced within the borders of that region/state. Alternatively, cost advantages may be obtained through evasion of taxes, since some of the smaller players might not be fully following the law compliant practices. Some of these would also not be champions of ethics and could reduce their internal costs by utilizing unauthorized labour at cheaper compensation levels.

Other non-ethical practices rather common in an E.M., thanks to legislations which do not guarantee adequate protection to intellectual property, give rise to the sprouting of counterfeit products. These would normally be produced by small manufacturers who specialize in copying successful products, sometimes operating across industries, thus producing from packaged water to snacks to even fake medicines. They may produce copycats which look similar to the original product for the colours of the packaging or have lookalike/sound-alike brandnames. At times such producers may manage to catch hold of the same quantities of rejected original wrapper of the product, maybe from the supplier's scrap yard, and use it to wrap their production. The most dangerous case for the original product is the complete copy of the brand, therefore a product which would appear exactly as the one manufactured by the real owner of it, including the statutory declarations and the address of the manufacturer. Such copies might be bought by consumers who genuinely believe they are the original ones, but they find a very low quality while using them. Similar incidents may lead to the loss of loyal consumers or even, in case the nature of the counterfeit is such to harm the user (low quality food, fake medicines), to the suing of the company owning the brand by the deceived consumer.

Due to the lapses in the legislations of many E.Ms, it is rather difficult to fight in an effective manner the counterfeits. The recommended action plan normally passes through the help of the local police which, following a court order previously obtained, will raid the premises of the out-of-law manufacturer, seize the stock, seal the operation and sometimes directly take the responsible to jail.[10] When such raids are successfully carried out, the spreading of the news of them through the local media will become an effective deterrent for other fake products manufacturers.

Other national or foreign players may be competing on the whole country's territory. They would normally have more ethic and fair practices than those mentioned earlier. However, since international companies also are often managed by local executives who may sometimes follow local practices, one should not rule out the possibility of border line behaviours by these players too. These may not be so direct and open as the cases previously mentioned, but may still be a source of threat and at times damaging for the company.

Such instances could be the launch of produces which share similar platforms (e.g., product benefit, positioning) with the ones marketed by the original owner. Depending on the legislation of the E.M. where this happens, there may be more or less successful tools of protection (e.g., common courts of law, advertising jury, etc.). Such cases could still fall within more or less fair competitive activities, happening in all countries but more frequent in emerging ones. Other instances, may be more subtle and insidious: this would be the case when, for instance, untruthful rumours are spread in the market and among local authorities in order to provoke their intervention and create troubles to the targeted competitor. Since in these markets it is relatively easy to convince unscrupulous officers, there might be instances when desperate players would not hesitate to use such practices in order to take advantage of setback caused by their actions.

More in general, in the legal and judiciary systems of the E.Ms it is likely to find gaps that could be used by aggressive competitors to gain advantages over more straight-forward players. Also from a marketing point of view, here it is not rare to find cases of irresponsible branding or advertising, carried out not only by local players, but sometimes also by local brand managers of MNCs, maybe by their own initiative and without the endorsement of the headquarter. Furthermore, being the cost of failure and brand building relatively low in these countries, marketers can be more daring and launch higher number of products, promotions or advertising campaigns.

The investment of excessive resources to defend the own market share by responding to those competitors with little chance of becoming major threat might become de-focusing and unnecessary work. On the other hand, ignoring a competitor who, despite its current small size, shows a continuous growth and aggressive ambitions may lead to an unforeseen loss of market share, at times difficult to recover.

Many examples can be quoted of such a mistake. In India, the local Unilever (Hindustan Lever Limited), for many years the largest consumer company in the country, lost in the span of two years many points of market share in the detergent market by not reacting to the entry of a low price local brand (Nirma) (see Chapter 4, Section 4.2.3). In China, Coca-Cola lost share to Wahana, a local competitor who had launched Feichang Cola at a lower price in low medium range supermarkets. Even in developed markets major players have made similar mistakes: in USA, for instance, General Motor initially refused to produce small cars and for this lost share to Japanese producers. So did Xerox when they refused to produce small copier machines, thus not regarding to the innovation introduced by canon.

In conclusion, a wise player will have to find the right balance between an over-reaction and a lack of attention towards the activity of smaller sized competitors. To do so, a continuous monitoring of the competitive environment will be necessary to ensure that all new challengers are carefully evaluated and pre-emptive measures to possible threat are timely implemented.

3.2.4 Infrastructure

In the previous chapters we have repeatedly maintained that one of the difficulties encountered in setting up a business in an E.C. is the lack of adequate infrastructures. In this section we shall try to give a more detailed idea of the level of development of some of the infrastructure that one can expect to find in the BRIC countries, and particularly in transport and communication.

Roads, railways, waterways, harbours and airports constitute the transport network of a certain country, which is quantifiable with indicators that give a general idea of its development at a certain date. However, when dealing with E.Cs, only a much more detailed analysis, and sometimes only the physical presence and direct experience in the country, can actually reveal the real conditions of what appears in the statistics.

To give an example of this, available data on Brazil may state that the highway network consists of 1.7 million kilometres, of which approximately 80 per cent of these are under the jurisdiction of the Municipalities, some are under the states and some under the Federal jurisdiction. A very large number of kilometres of highways may give the idea that the road infrastructure is good, thus the movement of goods through trucks should not constitute a problem. However, the reality may be different: what is classified as a highway in that country would be considered as an inter-regional road in a European country, where highways have usually at least three lanes for each direction, controlled access and allow an average speed of 100 kilometres/hour. Conversely, in the country under consideration, the so-called highway would be typically much narrower, with a relatively controlled access, sometimes passing through towns or villages and allowing an average speed of over 60 kilometres/hour.[11] As a matter of fact, out of the huge number of kilometres of highways indicated in Brazil, only 95,000 kilometres are paved. Also, a study conducted by the Confederation National of Transportation in 2001 stated that at that time only 2.3 per cent of the highways were in very good condition and over 66 per cent of them were deficient.

In a country like Russia, the total number of kilometres of the highway network may seem relatively high (over 530,000 kilometres), also due to the large size of the country, however, because of the weather conditions, an important percentage of the same may remain inaccessible for many months in a year.

Bric Countries: Infrastructure Scenario

In China, we find a highway network similar to the one of Brazil in terms of kilometres, but in this case the number of paved kilometres is four times that of Brazil. Despite this, even in this case less than 25 per cent of the total network is paved. In India, we find the largest highway network of the four considered countries, with over 2.5 million kilometres, of which over 56 per cent are paved (see Table 3.1). Such a huge network, mostly a heritage of the British administration, could lead to think that the transportation on the road is the most developed among the countries being analysed. A direct comparison with China, would on paper see India much ahead, with a total highway network which is four times that of China, and a total paved network which is 3.7 times that of the neighbouring country. However, once again the numbers prove to be highly deceiving. A visit in the coastal areas of China, which constitute the areas where most of the population lives, would reveal that the highways here are dramatically better than those in the corresponding

TABLE 3.1 TRANSPORTATION

| | Highways (kms) | | Railway | Waterways | Ports/harbour | Airports | |
	Total	Paved	(kms)	(Kms)	no.	Total no.	With paved runways
Brazil	1,724,929	94,871	29,412	50,000	9	4,136	698
Russia	537,289	362,133	87,157	96,000	33	2,586	577
India	2,525,989	1,448,655	63,230	14,500	8	333	234
China	1,765,222	395,410	71,898	121,557	7	472	383

Source: www.theodora.com (indicated source: CIA World Fact Book, 2005).

areas in India. Almost all the highways starting from the metro cities (e.g., Beijing, Shanghai, Shenzhen) and most of those in the developing regions (e.g., Guandong) are very similar to the Western concept of highways, with controlled access, adequate width of the lanes in each direction and good quality of the pavement. At the moment when we write, comparable quality of highways in India, can be found only in two main stretches, namely the Bombay–Pune one in the west of the country and some parts (less than 100 kilometres) of the Delhi–Jaipur highway. The vast majority (almost totality) of the Indian highways have no controlled access, narrow lanes and poor pavement quality. Also, most of them run across towns and villages, and they are prone to all the inconveniences of the town roads (traffic lights, traffic jams, slow moving stretches, etc.)

Even in the extra urban Indian areas, the situation is not much better: roads are populated by all sorts of inhabitants apart from motor vehicles. Cyclists, tractors, three wheelers and all kinds of vehicles circulate on the Indian highways, but many others use these roads for their daily needs, and it is rather frequent to find also horses, camels and even elephants pulling carts loaded with goods or passengers. Therefore, there is hardly any safety on the roads and the average possible speed is below 50 kilometres per hour.

However, what we describe is a picture at a given point in time, which could rapidly change in the years to come, considering the remarkable level of foreign investments flowing into these countries and the stated plan of the respective governments to develop the infrastructures.

China represents a vivid example of how quickly roads and communications can improve if there is a strong will in the country to do so and the executive power has the capability to enforce its decision (see Box 3.9). During the last two decades the face of China has completely changed and a visitor who had been to Shanghai during the eighties and comes back there now would possibly think he is in a different city. Apart from the earlier mentioned quality of the roads, China has the highest percentage of airport paved runways (more than 80 per cent) of the BRIC countries, as well as over 260 million of fixed telephone lines and as many mobile lines (see Table 3.2), thus 5.4 times the number of fixed lines of India (the second of the countries in number of fixed lines) and 5.8 times the number of mobile lines of Brazil, the second largest BRIC country for mobile phones. While the number of internet hosts is relatively low (approximately 160,000 at the moment of the statistics mentioned earlier), also possibly due to some restrictions imposed by the authoritative government, the number of internet users at the mentioned moment was close to 100 million, thus five times those of India at the corresponding time.

TABLE 3.2 COMMUNICATIONS

	Telephones (mio)		Television broadcast stations	Internet (mio)	
	Fixed	Mobile		Hosts	Users
Brazil	38.8	46.4	138	3.16	14.3
Russia	35.5	17.7	7306	0.60	6.0
India	48.9	26.2	562	0.09	18.5
China	263.0	269.0	3240	0.16	94.0

Source: www.theodora.com (indicated source: CIA World Fact Book, 2005).

Note: Telephones and internet data refer to the years 2002 and 2003, and may be different from the current scenario.

Box 3.9 THE EXPANSION OF CHINA RAILWAY NETWORK

'Daqin railway, which is set to become the first railway company to trade shares on a mainland stock exchange, said it seeks to raise as much as 15 billion Yuan, or USD 1.9 billion, in an initial share sale in Shanghai.

...Daquin, Guangshen Railway and other rail companies are tapping the capital markets to finance their expansion after China's two decades of economic growth, averaging 9.6% a year, boosted demand for cargo transport throughout the nation. Freight traffic on China railway network has increased by more than 60% since 1990, according to the World Bank. China's economic expansion has been clogging the country's railway networks with only less than 40% of the cargo demand being met...

The government plans to invest more than 160 billion Yuan this year to expand China's rail network, the most spent on railway infrastructure in a year, according to the Ministry of Railways'.

Source: Excerpts from an article by Jianguo Jiang and Tian Ying appeared on Bloomberg News and edited by the International Herald Tribune, 14 July 2006.

Among the BRIC countries, Brazil was the one who started developing its infrastructural communication technology during the eighties. The telecommunications monopoly was abolished in those years and a new legislation allowing private enterprises to bid for cellular licenses was approved. The process of privatization and de-regulation resulted in dramatic improvements in the quality of phone services. Other measures were successfully implemented to enhance the internet network infrastructure, particularly in the Brazilian business triangle (Sao Paulo, Rio De Janeiro and Minos Gerais), where high capacity fibre and broad bandwidth were installed. More recently the government has been seeking to improve the web usage spread also in low income areas, by launching the Universal Access Plan and through a project allowing free access to Internet kiosks in selected post offices in the main metro towns. As a result of these measures, the number of Internet users at the time of these statistics was almost comparable to that of India, despite the much lower population; this made Brazil the BRIC country with the highest percentage of Internet users.

The heritage of the past role as one of the two most powerful military nations of the world, is clearly reflected in the transportation infrastructure in Russia. The country has the largest railways network among the BRIC countries, with almost 90,000 kilometres of rails. Also the waterways are second only to China and close to 100,000 kilometres; the utilized harbours are 33, more than three times those of the second country. In this case, the communications infrastructures are lagging behind the other BRIC countries, both in terms of phones and also for the internet. However, the telephone system underwent significant changes in the nineties and today there are more than 1,000 companies licensed to offer communication services.[12] Progress is therefore being made towards building an adequate telecommunication infrastructure in line with the requirements of a market economy: however, there is still good scope for improvement.

3.2.5 Climatic Conditions

Over the centuries, many studies from scientists and economists have tried to establish a correlation between climatic conditions and economic development. By looking at the world map, it is rather immediate the observation that most of the developed countries lie in temperate zones, far from the extreme cold of the poles as well as from the hot and humid equatorial belt. Therefore, the reality of the world economic development provides a first empirical proof of the influence of the weather on the socio-economic life of the societies.

An implication of this is that most of the countries forming the subject of this book (non-fully developed countries) have difficult climatic conditions that will influence, in one way or another, the way of doing business within their territories. Forgetting to consider this in the initial business plan may lead to underestimation of the investments required or even to complete failure of the plan, when one of the elements of the marketing mix has been conceived in completely different weather conditions and replicated in an E.M.

Let us first examine the very cold countries. Some of these will be having snow and temperature below zero for many months of the year. The first consequences of this are the difficulties that a company will experience in moving its goods and having its people travelling in extremely cold weather. Often airports will be closed, roads or railways covered with snow and ice; sometimes the power generations or the communications may be affected by the very severe weather conditions and towns or even entire regions of the country would be isolated and cut out of the normal life for days or weeks.

In such circumstances, the distribution of goods to the retailers will be affected, with consequent out of stocks and loss of sales for the company. The supply chain might also be affected at the source, since some ingredients necessary for producing the finished goods may not reach the factory due to the roads conditions. A first general conclusion is that in a similar weather condition a company should plan to work with a higher level of stocks, both at the manufacturing (raw/packing materials) and at the distribution level (finished goods in the distribution centres or at the retailers point of sales). Also improving the sales and distribution costs would be the vehicles to be provided to the sales people in order to visit the clients and deliver the products: bicycles, motorbikes or three wheelers, very much common in temperate and hot countries, would not be usable in cold ones for the greatest part of the year. Alternatively, a company may have to consider providing cars sufficiently robust to withstand very low temperatures and icy roads, with clear implications on the fixed overheads of the distribution infrastructure. Even in this case, sales people may only be able to work for part of the day, since they may have to stop their visit when the sun sets and the temperature drops considerably.

The manufacturing operations would be affected by the severe cold too. The utilities to run a factory will have to be dimensioned on the peak low level of temperature, thus good enough to be smoothly working when the mercury reaches extreme low values (say minus 40 degrees). Some of the cold countries may even have rather warm, albeit short, summers (e.g., some regions of Russia reaching 30 degrees during the day time). In this case the factory utilities will have to be equipped to cope with a temperature range of 60/70 degrees, with evident consequence on costs of purchasing and operations. Energy consumption would be very high during the winter months, with influence on the variable cost of the finished product. The initial investment to set up a factory will probably be higher than in temperate climates, since provisions for weather proof structures and equipment, impacting on the fixed manufacturing overheads, will have to be included. Factories utilizing effluent treatment plants for outbound water will have to enclose them in structure to prevent the freezing of the same. Similarly, liquid ingredients utilized in processing the goods will have to be stored in adequate temperature so as to maintain the liquid states or be de-frozen before or during the production cycle. Some precautions will have to be taken while distributing liquid goods to the final point of sale. Higher costs of energy will also be incurred in heating the offices during most part of the year.

Opposite problems to those so far mentioned are experienced in very hot countries, often tropical or equatorial ones, where the average temperature exceeds 30 degrees through the year, with peaks at more than 45 and humidity level often above 90 per cent.

In such countries there would not be the problem of closure of roads for ice or snow, though the constant high temperature may eventually lead to more frequent road repairing, also due to the asphalt melting. Instead of high raw materials or finished products stocks to prevent losses of production/sales, the average level of goods, particularly finished products at retailer points, would be rather low and certainly lower than in cold weathers. The hot and humid weather negatively affects the shelf life of the products, particularly if stored in sub-optimal conditions like is the case in the smaller street kiosks or non air-conditioned outlets. Such shops represent the largest part of the retailers in E.Cs, where the modern distribution weight is often a fraction of that of the so-called *'mamas and papas stores'*. This largely affects the distribution of perishable goods, particularly those which need to be maintained in a cold chain (e.g., ice creams, frozen products, etc.). For this reason, in a country like India, where a universe of over three million outlets may appear, the theoretical distribution achievable for an FMCG item, products needing special storage conditions (e.g., chocolate) would have a maximum distribution basis of less than 10 per cent of the mentioned number and realistically even less than 5 per cent, according to the strength of the distributing company.

In hot weather countries, distribution of products can happen through cycles or motorbikes, but the high temperatures of the afternoon, or the heavy rains of the monsoon seasons, reduce the working hours and consequently the productivity of salesmen. The habit of the after lunch 'siesta' is not only a Mexican one but is rather common in many E.Cs, or at least in some regions of them (e.g., West Bengal, in the east of India).

Factories operating in similar climates would not need to scale their utilities for very wide range of external temperature, as mentioned for the cold countries. However, the air-conditioning to control the shop floor temperature and humidity will likely to have to work through the year with peak loads during the rainy seasons. During these seasons the effluent water treatment plants (which are usually built in the open with tanks and reactors exposed to the atmospheric agents) may receive shocks which would need time to recover and could create disturbance to the day-to-day operation. The continuous use of the air-conditioning, both in the factories and in the offices, could imply high energy costs. The products' recipes will have to be adapted to the climate: considering once again the above example of the chocolates, the melting point of these will have to increase versus the normal 35 degrees utilized in moderate climates. Consequently, a different combination of ingredients and higher melting point will give the chocolate a taste not comparable with that one could find in a temperate climate. Also, in order to protect the product from humidity and hot temperature, which represent a breeding field for bacteria, extra precaution should be taken for the packaging, which will need to be strong enough and possibly airtight. Cases of pest infestation are not rare in similar countries, and may create severe damages to the revenues and image[13] of the company selling the questioned product.

Apart from the direct impact on the business, climatic conditions influence the everyday life and habits of the people, their culture and their general attitude towards life. A general observation is that countries where the sun is shining for most part of the year have on an average a higher percentage of 'happy and content' people: this is irrespective of their income. To some extent, sometimes a higher income correspond to a lower level of general happiness, as surveys that found the South Americans to be among the happiest in the world seem to prove.

On the other hand, some other surveys recorded higher percentage of suicides among the Central/North European countries (e.g., Switzerland, Scandinavia), where the average per capita income is rather high versus the world median, but the weather is often cloudy and rainy, with few hours of sun and very short daylight in certain seasons.

Looking at the climate from another perspective, one can try to understand the impact of the increased business activities of the BRIC countries on the climate, rather than the influence of the same on doing business in the mentioned countries.

It is ascertained that the industrial growth which is one of the main drivers of the ascent of the BRIC countries to the world's attention, has consequences on the global environment and therefore, on the climate.

It is a fact that the main polluters are still the most industrialized Western countries. Only towards the end of the last century some major themes impacting the environment have been seriously considered in international forum, and documents like the Kyoto Protocol have stated important principles to limit the damage of careless exploitation of the world's natural resources. However, not all the participants have committed to adhere to that protocol: as a paradox, some of the major economic powers, and consequently those countries who take the highest toll on environment, have refused to stick to the main agreed measures to improve the world's health.

More recently, some of the countries who had been part of that forum have stated their intention to revise the final conclusions and produce another protocol to which also those who have not yet adhered should agree to participate. Whatever the revision may be, it would be fair that the E.Cs, which do not possess the advanced technologies of the developed ones to minimize the impact of their industrial activity, were provided with this know-how before being requested to respect standards, which were not respected by those Western countries during their developmental stage.

Having said this, among the BRIC countries the one which has showed the highest sensitivity towards a sustainable growth is by all means Brazil: it is not by chance that it is the country with the highest percentage of ethanol running cars of the BRIC (and possibly in the world). At the other extreme today is India, where the high population, the high illiteracy and poverty, and the rather obsolete industrial technologies make this country the most polluting (in relative terms) of the four. It is heartening to notice that after a number of ecological disasters, the Chinese Government seems to have finally started perceiving the importance of a more regulated industrial development (see Chapter 5, Section 5.1).

Notes

1. An important element to consider in the selection of the candidate is the overall cost of the children's education (sometimes very expensive in international schools in E.Cs.) as well as the family annual return tickets, sometimes as relevant as to become an important percentage (20 to 40 per cent) of the overall package.
2. Example of a group with such a policy could be Nestlé: in India for instance, at a certain moment they had more than 40 expatriates in the local subsidiary. At the same time, more than 70 Indian managers were posted in countries other than India.
3. Examples of this are the Italian-French company, S.T. Microelectronics, and also partly Microsoft and other telephone mobile technology designers.
4. In 2004, Cannes Advertising Film Festival, an Indian Creative Director from the local subsidiary of an international advertising agency was Chairman of one of the main Judging Committees and member of another important one.
5. Examples of this can be found in the 'punk' movement, borne in the UK and spread in many other countries since late seventies; more recently, the declaration of legal validity of the gay marriages.
6. In China, the concept is classified in 'lien' which could be explained as integrity and 'mein-stu'.

7. This is not necessarily true for some commodities (e.g. cocoa, coffee in Brazil), particularly in agricultural products.
8. If we consider labour as a supply, this is clearly not true for unskilled manpower; on the other hand, it may still hold true for highly skilled resources.
9. In case of scarcity of talent, the skilled resources command a high premium. This was the case, for instance, of bright marketing resources in China during the nineties. They would have salaries as much as double their colleagues of comparable levels in other departments (e.g., production).
10. In the countries where similar violations are considered criminal offenses subject to immediate imprisonment.
11. The speeds are quoted only as an example and may not reflect the reality of facts.
12. For details see www.theodora.com
13. A case of worm infestations happened in Cadbury in India in 2003, in some batches of its most popular chocolate brands. The company had to change the packaging material and add over-wrap packs. Press news reported a drop of over 30 per cent in their sales in the successive 18 months after the incident.

References

Capon, N. and W. Vanhonacker. 1999. *Asian Marketing Casebook*, Singapore: Prentice Hall.

Cavusgil, S.T., P. Ghauri and M. Agarwal. 2002. *Doing Business in Emerging Markets*, New Delhi: Sage Publications.

Conway. 1994. 'Expatriate Effectiveness: A Study of European Expatriates in South East Asia', *Strategies for Asia Pacific*. London: London Guildhall University.

Earley P.C. and E. Rosakowath. 2004. 'Cultural Intelligence', *Harvard Business Review*.

Goleman, D. 1995. *Emotional Intelligence*, USA: Bantam Books.

Hill, C.W. 2001. *International Business: Competing in the Global Marketplace* (3rd edition), Irwin: McGraw-Hill.

Kotler, P., S.H. Ang, S.M. Leong and C.T. Tan. 1999. *Marketing Management, An Asian Perspective*, Singapore: Prentice Hall.

Lasserre, P. and H. Schutte. 1995. *Strategies for Asia Pacific*, London: McMillan Press.

Mc Gregor, James. 2005. *One Billion Customers: Lessons From the Front Lines of Doing Business in China*, New York: The Free Press.

Porter, M.E. 1980. *Competitive Strategy*, New York: The Free Press.

Prahalad, C.K. and K. Lieberthal. 1998. 'The End of Corporate Imperialism', *0000Harvard Business Review*.

4

BUILDING THE BUSINESS MODEL

If a wolf bites you, it's acceptable; what is bothering is when a sheep bites you —J. Joyce

4.1 Entry Strategy: Trading or Manufacturing?

To gain that which is worth having, it may be necessary to lose everything else —B. Devlin

A company may decide to enter a potential E.M. with different approaches, depending on the reasons which have prompted the same to start the business in that market (see Chapter 1, Section 1.3) and also depending upon the objectives and strategies retained.

If the country was chosen as a manufacturing base, from which the finished products would be re-exported to other markets, the company will need to set up a factory; similarly if the choice was driven by the opportunity of exploiting the local resources available (for costs of skills advantage). On the other hand, if the entry was decided to service the local market, the company may decide to do it through trading, therefore by importing the products in the country and marketing them there; however, also in this case it may decide to set up a local manufacturing plant in order to ensure a flexible and smooth offer to the market.

Often the import route is retained to test the country's potential before embarking in heavier investments. Products will then be imported from other factories and stored in a central warehouse, from which they will be transferred in the redistribution depots, which will eventually service the trade/clients in the different regions. Such an option permits a lean organizational structure of the local subsidiary, consisting of a small accounting department, some logistic resources, quality control team and the sales and marketing teams assisting the Country Manager. In case the company had decided to partner with one or more local distributors who would take care of marketing the products in the E.M., the local structure could actually be even smaller. However, this choice has implications to be evaluated in the light of the objectives set.

First, the E.M. could have import duties which will have to be factored in the final price of sales. Though in the recent years many E.Cs have gradually been reducing their tariffs, some of them might still have high duties, particularly for some industries they would like to protect. This could mean that the importing company may not be able to price the products at a level competitive vis-à-vis the local players, thus the sales potential could be reduced. While the imported products in E.Cs are often perceived of superior quality versus the locally manufactured ones and could sometimes command a premium price, on the other hand too high a differential would prompt many consumers to choose the local products.

Second, the import process may mean that between the order placed to the producer and the actual availability of the goods in the market may pass several weeks, unless the transport time is reduced through the utilization of air transport, at much higher freight costs. Also, custom clearance procedures are often long and troublesome in E.Cs, and the goods risk to be stationed in the custom warehouses for a long time if any officer decides to be 'particularly meticulous'.

To avoid that similar circumstances hinder the sales results, adequate levels of stock should be maintained in the local warehouses, leading to a higher working capital. Also, if any change to the products is required, the long lead time will reduce the flexibility of the operations, and may cause a delayed response to the market needs.

Therefore, promotional activities on the imported products to be communicated through flashes on the packaging material will need to be planned long time in advance, so as to allow the manufacturing country to procure the changed packaging material, run the required production and ship it to the country that had ordered it. Trading companies sometimes decide to gain flexibility by importing the standard products and re-packing (when possible) in the E.Cs or stickering them with a label indicating the informa-tion required by the local laws.

Deciding to set up a manufacturing location in an E.M. (see Box 4.1) is certainly a much more complex alternative, implying higher investments in fixed assets, the creation of a larger organizational structure and an overall higher risk, also proportional to the political stability of the country. This route is usually decided when a company foresees a long-term potential in the country and is therefore ready to invest time and resources to build up an infrastructure allowing to service the market in a more flexible manner. In this case the production could easily be adapted to the local requirements and not depend on the constraints (production capacity, needs of standardization, etc.) of a remote manufacturing location. The response time to the demand of the local market will certainly be shorter and the local marketers will have the opportunity of changing the product or packaging characteristics according to the results obtained. Possible custom duties on the imported finished products will be avoided, with the consequent savings on the costs and the opportunity of pricing the products at competitive market levels.

Box 4.1 Elements to Help Select a Manufacturing Location

- Availability of land or ready-made building to rent;
- Lead time to obtain land permits and operating licenses;
- Cost of building;
- Availability of fiscal incentives and duration of the same;
- Availability and costs of skilled labour;
- Unionized or union free environment and flexibility of labour laws;
- Availability and cost of power, water;
- Conditions of infrastructure: site close to main roads, access roads, distance from r.   .ays/ports/airport, fixed telephone lines;
- Proximity of main suppliers;
- Availability and costs of the main raw and packaging materials;

(Box 4.1—continued)

(*Box 4.1—continued*)

- Possible trade agreement with neighbouring countries and effective functioning of the same;
- Availability and proximity of housing facilities for employees;
- Experiences of other companies who have set up operations in the area.

However, the process of building a factory in an E.C. may be long and troublesome, and requires commitment and patience. Not rarely has it happened that companies that had started the project and sometimes even the construction, because of the difficulties, delays and frustrations experienced have eventually decided to go back on their decision, sometimes after having invested a large amount of resources. Starting from the initial phase, which could be the acquisition of the land on which to build the factory, or an already existing building, the company may find it difficult to get a 'clean property title', since the records on the estate may not be reliable or at times not even available. Once the land (or the building) is secured, the approval and licenses for the new projects will have to be obtained. Some of the same will be issued by Central Government authorities (e.g., Ministry of Industry, Ministry of Health, etc.) and some will have to be provided by local bodies at regional, municipality or sometimes village level. In similar cases the approval may not be depending on the content or formal exhaustiveness of the documentation submitted and taxes paid, but rather on the chance of finding the right person to interact with. This one may be willing to facilitate the process, sometimes in view of the possible advantages he might see in the upcoming project for the interests of his community, or maybe for his personal one.

If the factory is finally built and the various licenses to operate have been obtained, in the process of recruiting the needed workforce it may frequently have to face the request of local politicians to hire a large number of people recommended by them. If also this stage is overcome without major negative consequences and the production can start, the regular inspection of central and local authorities may still represent a possible source of hassles to be budgeted for the time and effort required. The hiring of an experienced Factory Manager, familiar with the local working environment, is crucial to ensure a smooth running of the operations.

While setting up a local factory in the E.Cs, companies would normally try to limit the entity of their fixed investments by sending relatively old machineries with low residual book value.[1] They would initially start with a limited number of relatively easy to operate production lines, in order to adequately train the local technicians on each of them and subsequently import more advanced machineries.[2]

The manufacturing route will therefore provide flexibility and duty saving, but will also add complexity and overhead expenses. An in-between solution, combining some advantages of the trading option to some others of the local manufacturing is the third party production. Such a choice will avoid the risks of higher fixed investments while considerably shortening the lead times vis-à-vis the import. The possible negative sides of such an alternative, which can be an intermediate step towards the decision of own local manufacturing, could be the lack of complete control of the production quality as well as the passage of know-how and recipes to the local partner, who could use the same to produce for some competing companies or even start producing his own competing product. An adequately structured contract with all the due legal protection may ensure a certain degree of protection, but not a foolproof one, given the uncertainty of the legal framework common to the E.Cs.

4.2 Engineering the Marketing Mix

Learning is about more than simply acquiring new knowledge and insights; it is also crucial to unlearn old knowledge that has outlived its relevance. Thus, forgetting is probably at least as important as learning —**G.R. Blair**

4.2.1 Product and Packaging

We dealt in an earlier chapter with the opportunities of utilizing the E.Ms as a low cost off-shore production base. A few years ago this was the common way for MNCs to participate in the economies of these countries.

At times, companies would see some tactical opportunity to also service the local market, while producing for other developed countries in the same. In this case, the company would probably try to use the same export product for the local market, sometimes changing the label if required by law, or just adding a few lines in them, may be through stickering or flashes on the secondary packaging. If they experienced that there could be a certain potential for the brand to increase its sales they would also consider some promotional support, possibly without producing any new commercial but by utilizing the one used internationally. At most this would be dubbed in the local language; but only if it was proven that only a marginal percentage of the country population could understand the language of the international version (most of the times English). 'The message goes well beyond the language' would quote some international brand manager to justify the saving foreseen in absence of a new modified/dubbed version of the product commercial. Even the pricing used for the local market would be much in line with the international positioning rather than with the consumer purchasing power.

Only during the nineties, MNCs have started perceiving the opportunity of approaching E.Ms with a different perspective. The poor results often obtained with the standardized approach, as well as the important market share of the local competitors, convinced progressively the headquarters about the opportunity of re-thinking the Brand Marketing mix according to the country where the same was (or would be) sold. From the theory of the maximized standardization stated by T. Levitt (1983) in the eighties, and the advantages both in terms of costs and of international brand identity, MNCs entering E.Ms steered the direction to a more flexible approach, passing through the strategy effectively summarized by the popular tag line, 'think globally, act locally'.

However, even from this perspective, sometimes the companies fell into the trap (and some of them still do even today) of assuming that the consumption pattern and the consequent life cycle of products in the local E.M. would have followed similar trends to those experienced in the country of origin, or in other developed countries where the same brand had been launched.

As a consequence of this, they utilized the E.M. as an opportunity to keep on running the old production machinery by selling old version/models of the products in the same. This happened rather frequently when the fixed investment to manufacture a product was high, and the sales in a less developed country would have provided an extension in the life cycle of the product and the life of fully depreciated machinery still in working condition. Such cases were rather common in the automotive sector, where old models were often launched in less developed countries. Similar examples are Peugeot models, specifically the 504, launched in North Africa; the past models of Volkswagen 'Beatle' still running in many South American countries; a model of an old Fiat 1100 produced in Italy in the fifties and sixties, still constituting the bulk of the taxis in some Indian cities.

Such an approach has been defined as the Global Product Life Cycle (Leonnet and Hennessey 1995), and assumes that, at any point of time, some cluster of countries will be at a certain phase of the product cycle, thus very similar products can co-exist in different markets at different stages of their life.

However, the market evolution patterns cannot be simply replicated in all the E.Ms, since the completely different environment conditions and the often very distinctive cultures co-existing in this would require a complete re-engineering of the marketing mix, in order to appeal to the bulk of the population of the country. If the companies target the appealing number of the emerging middle classes of the E.Cs, they shall adapt their brands to the needs and pockets of the local consumer. On the other hand, if their objective is to capture a limited number of the local elite consumers, i.e., the apex of the pyramid (see Chapter 1, Section 1.4), then they might afford to maintain the international positioning, in terms of brand identity; their target group would in fact be highly mobile and would recognize the brand tried or seen during some international trips. Also the pricing, usually premium in case of high image brands, could be maintained while targeting these consumers.

Approaches similar to the one described in the graph (see Figure 4.1), become more and more difficult to use in today's changed environment.

FIGURE 4.1 PRODUCT LIFECYCLE IN DIFFERENT MARKETS

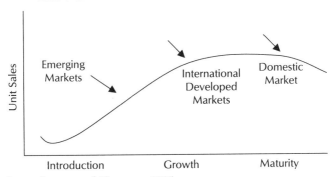

Source: Leonnet and Hennessey 1995.

Thanks to the faster information flow, consumers are much more aware of what happens in the world: they are likely to have seen better models or versions of the old products being marketed in the E.Cs, and depending upon the category, they could even be able to order the same via the Internet and get it delivered to their own doorstep. Also, competition from producers in the same E.Cs is more and more aggressive: some local players could be able to produce a version of the 'old' branded product marketed in the E.C. at lower costs and similar charactersistics. In these circumstances, many local consumers may prefer the locally branded (or even unbranded) version of the product to the branded old models available.

External conditions may force the international company manufacturing in an E.C. to change the formulation and engineering of its products. Availability of materials could be one of these limiting factors. Climatic conditions may be (and very often are) another major constraining variable. We mentioned earlier (Chapter 3, Section 3.2.5) the case of the chocolate distribution in countries with tropical weathers; even more problematic is to distribute ice creams in the same kind of countries. Opposite problems would be the same mentioned in categories in very cold weathers. For chocolates, the melting point of the same should be lowered against those used in tropical countries, in order to enhance their taste.

Climatic conditions influence also the specifications of the packaging materials. In tropical countries, food products need to be particularly protected from the humidity through strong and hermetically sealed packaging, so as to avoid or minimize the absorption of humidity which favours the growth of bacteria, thus shortening the product's shelf life.

In the confectionery segment, some products which can be sold in normal twist wrapped packing in moderate climate countries will need a completely different wrapper, possibly a metallic laminate, in a tropical country. Even renowned multinationals make mistakes in such conditions and risk to have to withdraw the products in the market due to the wrong packaging selection. One of these decided to launch in India a hard boiled candy, very attractive for its transparent appearance. To capitalize on this same competitive advantage (transparency) it was decided to pack it in a transparent though hermitically sealed pillow pack. Once the product remained in the market exposed to the heat and sun for a few days, it started melting and losing it's shape. The company had to withdraw it from the market and substitute it with a new version with a dark metallic wrapper.

The quality and attractiveness of the packaging material are often a decisive factor, not only to ensure the product quality, but also to generate additional sales: a common error that some companies may make is to provide cheap packaging in order to save costs, sometimes encouraged by the low quality of the local players. On the other hand, bright and well designed packaging would give a distinctive look to the product marketed, allowing it to stand out from the crowd of the average local players.

Apart from the external conditions which might force a company operating in an E.C. to change and adapt its products to the local environment, marketers and managers should always create local brands or modify global or international ones according to the need and requirements of the local consumers in order to fully exploit their sales potential.

Other local factors may influence and constrain the production and marketing in a country: among these are the local culture and religions. For instance, it is not possible (and sometime legally forbidden) to use pork based ingredients in Muslim countries, or cow based ones in Hindu states. Some specific product shapes may not be acceptable in certain cultures, and some other may have connotations fully contrasting with the product positioning (see Section 4.2.4 of this chapter).

The combination of product characteristics, not necessarily important in a developed country, could turn out to be a success factor in an emerging one. Philips Electronics introduced in China in 1994 a combination of video cassettes and CD player: although there was visually no market for a similar product in other Western countries, the Chinese consumers perceived it as good value for money and purchased over 15 million units (Prahalad and Lieberthal 1998).

In general, both product and packaging should be adapted to the local legal regulation and environment and, above all, to the target group's expectations: while this is clearly known and applied by companies in developed markets, until a few years ago it was not similarly implemented in the E.Ms. Today, without a conscious effort to effect such customization in these countries, a company would seriously limit the success of its products.

4.2.2 Distribution

Making sure that the products are widely available is a considerable challenge, particularly in those E.Ms where the infrastructures are not fully developed and often poorly maintained.

An international company entering an E.M. often chooses to rely on local distribution partners with expertise of the local environment and an existing network reaching part (or sometimes the whole) of the national territory.

In the very first stage of export to a new market and particularly to an emerging one the company would normally sell and distribute through one major importer with a network of sub-distributors and sales people. Often these importing companies also provide marketing services to the company, that may operate from a remote location, thus lacking commercial capabilities. When the decision of making a serious entry in the market is eventually taken and a local company is created with an organizational structure, companies decide often to progressively create their own distribution structure. As a matter of fact, particularly if the distributing partner is a large organization, international companies may find difficulties in ensuring that their guidelines are fully followed and their product receives the necessary attention to achieve the expected results. The usual conflicts mentioned in Chapter 2, Section 2.3 (e.g., long versus short-term objectives, expectations, etc.) may create disputes, at times compromising the relationship. Also, when the company has eventually decided to build its business in the E.C., the importer/ local super-distributor who would be likely to deal with several product lines from different principals, may not grant the expected focus on its imported product lines. It may therefore make sense to create one's own distributor network through a number of local dealers who would act as stock keepers and redistributors to the local trade.

There could be several criteria to select the local dealers/distributors, among which are, their knowledge and experience in the industry where the company operates, their financial solidity, their territorial reach, their own infrastructure as well as the possible exclusivity, or at least the agreement of not dealing with competitive products. Depending on the markets, there will be more or less availability of distributors with a high score in many of the mentioned parameters.

It is certainly of capital importance to carefully select the future dealers; a visit to their premises and a reference check with their clients or with other companies who might have had contacts with them will certainly prove beneficial to ensure a better choice. The thorough checking of their financial background is a mandatory step; a sound financial position will give the distributor the capability of operating without major restrictions. He will, in fact, be required to extend credit to some of the customers, thus absorb the possible risk implied by this. Also, he will have to be able to regularly pay for the goods purchased from the company, despite delays coming from the payments of their end buyers. Additionally, he will have to invest in the distribution infrastructure, by hiring people or buying vehicles, so as to ensure proper reach and be ready to adequately train his people, sometimes in cooperation with the principal. Through a visit to the distributor's premises the recruiting company will be able to ascertain that he has adequate space to store the products in the required hygienic conditions (e.g., products to be refrigerated), and also to check his internal resources (vehicles, people) and working systems.

Once the dealers are selected across the country's territory, the company will need to regularly communicate with them in order to make sure that the period-wise goals assigned to them are known and the agreed distribution policies are implemented as per the company's guidelines. Therefore, the company's sales people will need to have a systematic interaction with the distributors, work with them in the market and help them build confidence in the products. A prolonged lack of contact with them may result in the same not following the agreed guidelines, thus not delivering the expected results.

One basic reality to be remembered is that usually distributors tend to sell the easiest saleable products, thus those demanded by the retailers thanks to their popularity or to some promotional activities carried out by the markets. However, companies cannot always support all products with 'pull strategies' and sometime can only provide trade incentives for 'push activities'[3]. In this case, the capability of the distributors' sales people will prove handy to obtain at least short/mid-term results.

While it is important to keep distributors under a certain amount of pressure in order to make sure that they do not forget the company objectives (particularly when they deal with several principals thus distributing many product lines), a 'partnership' approach is recommended in order to maximize their effectiveness in the market. Therefore, it will not be useful to continuously push them to sell products without actual market potential: they will find it too hard and start 'dumping' the products (may be at lower prices) to achieve their objectives. An adequate support (sometimes even financial) and training will ensure a sound relationship which should maximize the mid-term results.

We indicated that industry expertise is one of the criterions to help select a capable distribution partner. While this normally ensures that the dealer knows the basic rules of selling and delivering a certain category of products and is familiar with their characteristics, it may turn counterproductive in certain cases. In fact, a distributor who has been in the industry for some time may have maintained a relationship with a previous principal operating in the same, possibly a competitor of the new one, and may pass to him important information about the sales policies carried out. Also, he may have acted as the dealer of a local player, thus learnt how to fulfill the expectations of small–medium-sized local companies. These may not be aligned with the strategies and objectives of an international company operating in the E.C. and it would possibly be more difficult to make sure that he 'unlearns' his previous ways of distributing to align his skills and infrastructure with the new guidelines.

It could, therefore, be advisable for the company to select distributors who have had previous experience with other international players, though operating in different industries.

The peculiarities of the retail structure of E.Ms play an important role in the distribution strategy to be retained. Typically in these markets the trade will be rather fragmented, with small corner shops and general merchants representing the majority of the outlets. Modern and organized retailing chains such as Wal-Mart, Carrefour would be only partly present, (see Box 4.2) if not at all. The specific country may, in fact, have laws forbidding Foreign Direct Investment in retailing.[4]

BOX 4.2 RETAIL GIANTS FACE CURBS ON EXPANSION

'The Ministry of Commerce has completed draft rules to regulate the expansion of large retails stores that might disproportionately affect foreign retailers, state media reported.

The regulations are awaiting final approval from the Cabinet, China Securities Journal reported. The rules would impose a slew of new restrictions on the building of large retail stores, which would also become subject to a public hearing process, the newspaper cited unnamed ministry sources as saying on Wednesday. The regulations would also require local governments to submit detailed commercial planning blueprints, a

---

(*Box 4.2—continued*)

(Box 4.2—continued)

> move aimed at avoiding the bunching of stores that may lead to excessive retail competition, the newspaper said.
>
> It said foreign chains such as Wal-Mart and Carrefour would be disproportionately affected by the new rules because most of the big new supermarkets and shopping malls in the mainland are built by international retailers. Many local retailers have expressed concern about the growing influence of foreign chains in the domestic market.
>
> Assistant Minister of Commerce Huang Hai was cited this month by local media as saying the new rules would apply the same standards to domestic and foreign companies.'

Source: The Standard, Hong Kong, 20 July 2006.

The presence of a large number of small outlets makes the distribution reach rather difficult and lengthy. On the other hand, the concentration of organized chains in developed countries allows a producer to obtain through a central contact the immediate presence in all the outlets of the chain, though at a certain agreed price to be paid to obtain the listing and the shelf space.

Apart from the reach of a vast number of outlets, requiring a capillary network not easy to build, particularly when the country territory is large and difficult to access, some other characteristics are typical of an E.M. with a highly fragmented trade structure. One of these is the limited capability of retailers to purchase when a company would expect to sell a large portfolio of products. The retailer will allocate to a certain goods category a limited amount of cash, and will thus buy only the products that he is rather sure to sell. A way to partly overcome such a handicap is a certain number of days of credit given by the distributors, so as to allow him to first sell the product delivered and later pay with the funds coming from the sales to the end consumers (or any other of his client, in the case of a wholesaler).

Another implication of a fragmented and unorganized trade is the limited space available to store and display the products, which could constrain the purchases or limit the products' sell out, particularly for impulse categories which need to be visible to stimulate the sales. A good help in this case is to provide products which have rationalized size and permit an effective storage. Also, in order to increase the visibility of their products, companies sometimes provide free of cost merchandising material that increase the shelf space of the retailer (floor stands, racks), while enhancing the display of their products. However, these are typically utilized from the retailer to hold several products and not necessarily only the brands of the company who had supplied them: a regular merchandising action is therefore, necessary to re-position the original product in the dispensers as well as to maintain the racks in good condition. In fact, they are often left out in the open, particularly in small outlets with limited space, and get dusty and dirty within a few days.

A third consequence of the unorganized and small retailers is the suboptimal storage condition of the products that particularly impact the food items and the perishable ones, and constrain the producer to recommend a shorter shelf life for the same. Sometimes it severely limits the width of distribution for those products that need special storage precautions (e.g., refrigeration).

Additional difficulties faced by the companies operating in E.Ms are associated to the scarcity of reliable market data to assist in formulating distribution strategies. On one hand, the statistics on the existing outlets are difficult due to their large numbers; on the other, their life span is relatively short since small kiosks may open and close in short time, and some of them may change locations according to the selling opportunity of a particular period (e.g., village celebrations attracting a large number of people as well as temporary outlets).

The lack of adequate infrastructure such as roads and transportation obliges company wanting to operate in an E.M. with a large territory to create some intermediate warehouses: here their goods can be stocked in order to reduce the time of service to distributors covering locations far from the main warehouse (or the local factory). In fact, the quality of the roads and sometimes the vehicles used to transport lengthens the delivery time. In Nigeria, for instance, a country which is spread over 2000 kilometres from east to west, a delivery starting from Lagos, almost in the extreme south-east of the country, may take as long as eight days to reach the north-western border.

In order to overcome similar shortcomings, some MNCs have decided to build their own transportation infrastructure: this was the case of Nestlé, that acted so in order to join farms of 27 villages to its factory collection point in China's northern Heilongjiang province (Kotler et al. 1999).

Distribution in E.Ms represents, therefore, an entry barrier for international companies that decide to start operating in one of them (see Box 4.3) as well as a limiting factor for those companies that already have operations in them. The complexity of achieving a national distribution in an E.M. must be carefully considered while structuring the other variables of the marketing mix.

Box 4.3 WAL-MART GROWS BOLD IN CHINA

Shenzhen, China—Wal-Mart plans to hire 150,000 people in China over the next five years, five times the number it currently employs here, as it prepares for a major store expansion.

Joe Hatfield, Chief Executive of Wal-Mart Asia, who has worked at the world's biggest retailer for more than 30 years and was its first employee in China in 1994, said on Sunday that the company planned to open 20 stores in the country this year and was racing to train more staff so that it could speed up growth.

'We're really going to ramp this up,' Hatfield said in an interview while touring stores in Shenzhen, Wal-Mart's China Headquarters.

The Bentonville, Arkansas-based retailer currently has 56 stores in China, putting it behind other global chains such as France's Carrefour, which had 78 at the end of 2005.

Wal-Mart did not even register enough sales to crack the top 30 on the Commerce Ministry's list of the biggest retailers in China, released last month.

That looks set to change.

'We're going to be growing in all directions,' Hatfield said, adding that new stores were planned for both the major metropolises and the smaller cities.

Wal-Mart's China operations could be as big as its U.S. business in 20 years, Hatfield said. Wal-Mart's 3,700 U.S. stores generated 80 per cent of its USD312 billion in sales for the latest fiscal year.

Wal-Mart's stores in China can draw 1.2 million people per month. The retailer employs about 30,000 people in China.

Source: Excerpts from *The Moscow Times*, 21 March 2006.

4.2.3 Price

Each marketing mix variable contributes to the success of a product and it is rather difficult[5] to isolate the effect of one from the other so as to weigh their ultimate impact on sales. However, in the context of the E.Ms the role of pricing is certainly crucial and the success or failure of the product is much more dependent on the right pricing choice here rather than in developed countries. This is mainly a consequence of the market structure which in the E.Cs typically has a very high percentage of the population with a low dispensable income and consequently much aware of the allocation of the same among the needed goods or services. In general, consumers in the E.Cs are more price conscious than their counterparts in developed ones; from a microeconomic perspective, their demand curve is more elastic and sensitive to even small price differences.[6]

As per the marketing manuals, the process of setting a pricing policy has different steps, starting from the product strategy (e.g., maximizing sales, growth or profit) and passing through the estimate of the demand curve and the recording of the direct competitors' prices. In E.Cs marketers will start facing difficulties from the very first stage, due to the absence of a reliable market data both on the demand and sometimes on the competitors, particularly when these are local unorganized players. It may also happen that the product to be launched does not have a direct competition at the time of the launch, since the player is a first mover (see Chapter 2, Section 2.2) in the market. In this case, the pricing strategy of possible substitute categories will have to be considered, since the new launched product will eventually indirectly compete with products with similar functions, though with different characteristics (e.g., *paan*—beetel nut with spices in a leaf versus chewing gum, or *bidi*—a mixture of tobacco and herbs in a leaf versus cigarettes in India).

At times, completely different products may experience competition with each other, when they target the same consumers' share of money, because of the mentioned low disposable income. A street worker in a tropical country may have to decide whether to buy a glass of cold water from the nearby kiosk after his working hours or to spend the same amount to buy one cigarette.

Once the market pricing structure is known, the marketers will have to decide the pricing methods, keeping in mind their cost structures. Also in this case, a thorough analysis of the competitors' cost structures will help understand how much efficient the local production could be and explore new avenues in cost saving. Cost-ing is typically the first base to build the market price, though the different methods do not necessarily utilize the mark-up as the only way of fixing the final price.[7]

The last fine-tuning of the pricing structure is usually done taking into account some psychological elements (e.g., 999 instead of 1000) or the influence of other internal and external factors. Among these, a very important one may be the coinage available, which could eventually determine the prevalent market price, sometimes becoming an unsurmountable road block to the business plan profitability. This happens particularly in the FMCG sector of the E.Cs and is again driven by the low consumer purchasing power. Examples of this could be the 1 RMB price point in China or the 50 paisa (half rupee) price point in India. The latter has the physical constraint caused by the fact that the 50 paisa coin is the smallest coinage widely available in the market.

Historically products like candies have been sold at this price point in single piece packs. Companies have not been able to increase the price of the same for the last several years, since the next available price point would be Re 1, and this would mean doubling the price. Considering the high elasticity of the demand in this country, such a price increase, if not followed by the entire market, could result in a dramatic loss of sales (as high as 80 to 90 per cent of the total) for the company who would dare to experiment.

Price wars are always detrimental to business, but they could be particularly damaging in the case of E.Ms. Unless the company that is entering the market has the resources to maintain an aggressive level of pricing in the mid-term, it is not advisable to engage in a price battle which will eventually put out of business the weaker competitor, in the meantime drastically reducing the category profitability.

A similar instance happened in Hong Kong in the newspaper market. Here an initial duel between two of the daily newspapers, caused by the launch of one (*Apple Daily*) of them priced well below the then prevailing market price (5 HKD) at 2 HKD, provoked the reaction of the other (*Oriental Daily News*). The event sparked a chain of reaction from the other newspapers, resulting in a price war, which eventually caused the reduction of the price of the weekly magazine too (from 18 HKD to 8 HKD). The toll of the same was the closing of the operations of nine of the publications (Kotler et al. 1999).

However, even if a price war is mostly better avoided, at times, the lack of reaction to a competitive move could be equally dangerous, particularly when a potential player significantly reduces his price level in a very elastic market such as an E.M. could be.

Once again the example of this is found in India, during the nineties, in a market dominated for many years by the major FMCG company in the country, Hindustan Lever Limited (HLL), subsidiary of Unilever, having the highest market capitalization in India. Among many other industries, HLL was the undisputed market leader in detergents, when a local company, Nirma, entered the market at a price much lower than their brand. There was no initial reaction to the launch, and Nirma managed to capture a significant market share in a relatively short time, also thanks to an innovative radio campaign. When HLL realized the significant gain of the challenger, they eventually lowered their price, but in the meantime many customers had shifted to the local brand, and the share lost was never really recovered.

In the E.Cs price is possibly the most important variable of the mix, with strong influence on the remaining variables as well as on the overall product image. The initial fixation of the launch price can determine the success or the failure of a launch. However, an adequate pricing strategy cannot remain unchanged during the time and depends on a number of internal and external factors. A mistake in the strategy, particularly in highly price sen-sitive markets, can lead to drastic loss of sales and some-times to the closing of operations.

4.2.4 Advertising and Promotion

Among the different variables of the marketing mix, the promotional one is maybe the only one not strictly indispensable in an E.M.

In fact, we mentioned how sensitive these markets are to the right pricing and how difficult it is to achieve an acceptable distribution reach in the same. The product quality in any market is a pre-requisite for a long term sustainable success. On the other hand, provided that the rest of the marketing mix is well studied and implemented, a product has good chances to obtain a reasonable level of sales in an E.M. with hardly any promotional support. This clearly depends on the market situation, but particularly where the level of consumers and products sophistication is low and the competition is not particularly aggressive, good quality products with the right price and a fair distribution have chance to earn their living despite marginal investments to promote their sales.

In such circumstances, companies use, for instance, an aggressive trade pricing in order to push the product on the shelves, and leave to the retailers, to whom they have granted a generous margin, the task to promote the sale of their products. Sometimes they provide minimal support through Point of Sales (POS) materials or some other time through other activities aimed at stimulating the trial (e.g., sampling or introductory offers). Once the sales start to take off, they may decide to re-invest part of the realizations in promotions and maybe some advertising, or just let the word-of-mouth spread and generate additional demand.

Such an approach is a possible way of launching a product with limited resources and risks and may work in the mentioned circumstances, though it would certainly take time before the whole potential market comes to know about the launch. In the meantime, some competitors may react with a similar product and decide to support it with advertising investments: in this case, the sales of the original product may never realize their full potential. A strategy which had been conceived to save resources would then end up compromising the success of a potential product.

Therefore, even in an E.M. an adequate investment to promote the brand's sales helps to accelerate their development and maximize their potential. What is 'adequate' depends on many factors, among which the penetration of the media in the target country, the costs involved, the level of advertising and promotion spending of the competitors and the overall level of investments and advertisements clutter in the market. According to the characteristics of these factors, a company may decide to invest the entire budgeted amount in above-the-line initiatives, and particularly in one media (e.g., TV); alternatively, they could decide for a 'push strategy' and invest most of their resources in below-the-line activities. Often a balanced mix (70 per cent above, 30 per cent below) gives the best results.

The positive element to be considered while budgeting a promotional investment in an E.C. is that, normally, the costs of media is relatively low vis-à-vis the same in a developed country. Therefore, with reasonable amounts that would not even be the minimal entry threshold in a European country, a company could be able to buy media space for a decent campaign with good frequency and duration. The reach will depend on the media selection and its penetration among the target public. Then, if the company decides to invest behind the product, the amount of resources will not be particularly high, thus the risk implied would be limited.

A thumb rule to be used for existing brands is to fix the percentage of Advertising and Promotion (A&P) support within 10 per cent of the sales revenue. For a product being launched the percentage could be much higher, considering the likely low initial level of sales.

On the other hand, for a product approaching the maturity in its life cycle for which the company has decided to adopt a 'milking'[8] strategy, the percentage may then be much lower.

While selecting the positioning of one of its brand, a company will have to ensure that its relevance for the target group is retained as well as its acceptability in the country where it is used (see Box 4.4). Neglecting to check these points may translate into waste of resources and low return on the investments done: at times, it may also damage the company's image when the positioning and consequently the campaign utilized is considered offensive for the local cultures and values. This happened for instance in an Islamic country, when a beverages producer decided to print inside the cap of one of his alcoholic products the flags of the world countries in the context of an international promotional activity. One of the flags contained some lines from the Holy 'Quran' and the association between these and the alcohol was considered highly offensive by the Muslim community of a certain country: the promotion had to be stopped and the products present in that market withdrawn.

Box 4.4 UNITED AIRLINES ENTERS THE FAR EAST MARKET

United Airlines bought from Pan American 18 planes and the routes from US westward to Asian destinations in February 1986. They positioned themselves as the best carrier for the Orient, which seemed quite a relevant promise, given the past deteriorating service of Pan American, and the 'low frills' service in the North-west. However their communication turned out to be highly over-promising vis-à-vis the reality, both because of

---

(*Box 4.4—continued*)

(Box 4.4—continued)

the not respected schedules (frequent delayed and cancelled flights) and for the rather poor service level, on-board and at the time of departure (e.g., long lines at the check-in). In time, the service improved, but other mistakes were made in their approach to the Eastern markets. In a presentation to some Japanese executives they showed an incomplete map of the country; they decided to have their in-flight hostesses wearing white carnations, which are considered not auspicious in some Asian countries; once they printed an ambiguous headline in their in-flight magazine, stating 'Paul Hogan Camps It Up for Australia', featuring a story about the actor P. Hogan (Crocodile Dundee), without realizing that the word 'camp' is an Australian colloquialism for homosexual behaviour.

Source: Hendon 2001.

More in general, MNCs entering E.Cs tend to assume that their international positioning would also work in these markets. Not often this is true, and after years of poor results, they have eventually started realizing that adaptation to the local culture works much harder than international standardization. Also in this case, there could be exceptions, particularly for high image brands (e.g., Bulgari, Chanel) targeting very selective niches. However, when the general public is considered, as the majority of the cases in the FMCG, a positioning adapted to the local habits and values will have much better chances to succeed.

As far as consumer and trade promotions are concerned, the positive side of operating in E.Cs is that the consumers (or trade) would have typically had a lower exposure to the latest fashion or high-tech gadgets flourishing in more developed markets and would thus, have lower level of expectations. Therefore, also in this case the promotional expenses could be lower than those necessary in more developed markets. Additionally, in some E.Cs countries (e.g., China, Malaysia) the cost of promotional items such as toys or household tools which could be used for consumers in packs or trade loads would normally be much lower than in developed countries; this would contribute to a reduced amount of resources necessary for an effective promotion. Among the lower expenses often included in the Advertising and Promotion budget will also be the listing fees for the Organized Trade, given the scarce presence of the same in many E.Cs. A further advantage could be the use of border line promotional claim, since the consumer associations are not normally particularly active here, neither the consumer protection legislation is.

However, some form of promotions which are often used in developed markets are not necessarily feasible or effective in the changed context of an E.M. This is sometime due to the infrastructure which may be not enough developed to support a certain initiative (e.g., direct marketing actions through the mail when the post system is highly inefficient). Some other time the structure of the distribution channels is such that it 'filters' some consumer promotion, preventing the promotional item to reach the final consumer. In other circumstances, it is the same consumer who reacts in an unexpected way and changes the rationale of the promotional mechanism. Given below are some examples from the Nigerian market which will help in understanding such circumstances.

- A renowned MNC operating in the market decided to promote its main product through a consumer promotion which added a sample of another popular brand to the main product in a bundle pack. The Brand Manager who went to visit the market to understand how effective the promotion was, could not find the bundle pack in the market. On closer examination he realized that the bundle had been opened and the free samples were being sold in the market, rather than being given for free with the original product.

- Another MNC dealing with food products tried to use a 'collect and win' scheme to promote the sale of a product. The consumer who would send a given number of covers of the container in which the product was sold would participate in a contest to win appealing prizes. While a high number of covers reached the Company after a few weeks from the start of the scheme, the total volume of sales was not actually increasing. A closer investigation in the matter revealed that in the towns where the promotion was running, some teams of boys had been hired to search in the garbage outside the residential areas, collect the covers and bring them to some designated person, who would complete the application and send them to the Company.

- Several companies tried 'scratch and win' consumer promotions, with cards inserted in the secondary packaging of the products, or sometimes given to the distributors so as to be handed over to the retailers, who should give them to the consumer purchasing a certain product. Marketing researches revealed that only very few consumers had the opportunity of experiencing the promotion: the cards had in fact been previously scratched at some stage of the distribution chain.

4.2.5 Public Relations

Public Relations (PR) have only been considered part of the Marketing Mix since the last two decades and are still one of the most under-utilized tools very often neglected by marketers. Even in developed markets PR are rarely given the importance they deserve, as a very versatile, credible and cost-effective way of communicating.

In E.Ms, where at times, companies erroneously tend to limit their marketing investments, PR would not appear among their priorities, thus would often be forgotten. On the other hand, it is particularly in these markets that an adequate attention to PR would allow to achieve results that no other marketing effort could deliver.

Already during the initial phase of establishing a venture in an E.C., companies may be confronted with a number of obstacles, legal and administrative, which sometimes only an effective lobbying activity with the local institutions may help to overcome.

Box 4.5 FDI IN RETAIL IN INDIA

Despite the progressive opening of many sectors to Foreign Direct Investments in India, one of those which are encountering a strong opposition is the retail one.

The highly fragmented retail universe (over 3 million of outlets) in the subcontinent represents a source of income for millions of households, and consequently a huge reservoir of votes for the local politicians. The current ruling coalition, enjoying the external support of the Communist Party, has stated since the beginning of their mandate the willingness to start opening the industry to foreign investors, but has had to cope with the pressure of their allied forces as well as that of the

---

(Box 4.5—continued)

(*Box 4.5—continued*)

retailers associations, who strongly oppose any opening towards that direction.

However, during the visit of an American delegation in 2004, rumours started spreading in the media about talks between representatives of the two countries discussing the opening of the retail sector to foreign investors. Behind the talk was clearly the lobbying activity of Wal-Mart, the largest world retailing chain that had been studying the Indian market for some time and had shown a definite interest in stepping in.

As a result of these, during the following months the Indian Government released the news that an amendment to the legislation on retailing was being studied and a phased opening of the same to foreign investors could be imminent. At the beginning of 2006, the first change in the legislation was eventually approved and the Single Brand International Retailers were allowed to detain up to a certain percentage in joint ventures with local partners.

Also, in order to expedite the procedures to create a local company, or to get the necessary approval required for trade or manufacturing in the country, a good relationship with the local bureaucrats can play an important role. To establish such rapport, the help of local agencies, can be sought, exploiting their experience and the network of knowledge. By appointing them as facilitators in their approach to the new market, international companies will save time and hassles often and minimize the frustration of long processes with poor outcomes. Many MNCs follow this route, utilizing the help of high level consultants (retired government officials, top-level businessmen) who are at times retained in their Board of Directors as a link with the local establishment.

The interaction with local authorities continue throughout the life span of the operations of the investors: careful PR and lobbying actions are sometimes required in order to avoid unpleasant surprises (e.g., the sudden change of a law, the creation of new restrictive measures for the industry or ambiguous taxes). The levels of interaction go from the highest (e.g., Central Government, top bureaucrats) to the lowest (e.g., local inspectors, neighbouring villagers in case of industrial set-up). Goodwill may be created through business lunches, invitation for events, invitation to visit the company's factory and offices and even sometimes with just personal courtesy visits.

Once the company business grows, its visibility and the expectations of the local communities increase. Global players such as renowned MNCs are requested to contribute to the social welfare of the local stakeholders (see Chapter 5, Section 5.3). Media is interested to find out about the company, its strategies, its results and the possible future plans, particularly those impacting the economic and social environment.

During the interaction with the media, it is useful to remember that in the E.Cs, journalists or anchormen are not always full-fledged professionals. Therefore, if on one hand, they are easier to handle and less demanding, on the other, the company spokesperson will have to make sure that they are driven in the right direction to ensure correct reporting of the data shared. Very often, data are misquoted, sometimes grossly different from reality and with negative consequences for the company's image. In some other instances, the reporters may almost completely forget the main piece of news that the company was willing to communicate and give prominence to other information they consider more interesting, which were hardly discussed during the meeting with the spokesperson. It is also to be remembered that media is less regulated in these countries: they can thus dare more and potentially be more dangerous and harmful.

Public Relations campaigns utilizing the electronic media and press may not be particularly effective for FMCG companies targeting low S.E.C. groups[9] (i.e., C and below). This is due to both the relatively low penetration of the media and the limited literacy of some of these countries (sometime not reaching 70 per cent of the adult population). However, the cost of PR campaigns could be rather low, often a small fraction of that of an advertising campaign.

Companies may decide to go for Corporate PR or Brand PR: the former campaigns may be particularly useful at the initial stage, when the venture needs to gain visibility vis-à-vis the local institutions; they may become crucial in case of market incidents reported by the Press and affect the general image of the company. This may happen for real facts (products contaminated or with structural defects) or for rumours spread in the market not responding to reality. These are the cases when the importance of PR is maximum and an adequate use of this tool may make the difference between a limited damage with a prompt recovery and a permanent loss of image and sales leading to the shut down of the operations. However, if such crisis possibility is not well prepared during non crisis period, PR may end up doing more harm than benefit to the company (see Box 4.6).

Brand PR is used to enhance the Brand equity. Sometimes it becomes necessary, when the local laws or culture do not permit direct advertising campaigns (e.g., cigarettes, contraceptives). If properly implemented it

Box 4.6 SPREADING OF RUMOURS: HOW TO REACT

- Give the facts about the problem to everybody in your firm. Involve the rank and file. Gain their support for your action. Have them form booster clubs. Set up employee rallies. Have your low-level employees available for media interviews.
- Take a quick survey to find out the demographics of your biggest rumour-spreaders so you'll know what media, geographic regions, and spokesmen to hit the hardest.
- Decide what points to refute, but never deny more than what's in the rumour—why call attention to more things that can hurt you?
- Concentrate on aspects that are unfair, untrue and unjust (or un-American, un-Canadian, un-British, or whatever nation you're in)—whatever's against people's sense of fair play. Don't play up the theme, 'My Company is suffering.' Nobody cares if you're suffering or not. They care about themselves and how the rumour affects them.
- Some experts think you should call a press conference, while others don't. Those who don't like conferences think you no longer have control over who hears the rumours and facts once the media has the information. I don't think this is a strong enough argument. I share the opinion of those who support press conferences—when the rumour becomes news, it's shared by the whole population and so the rumour-mongers will get no more thrill from spreading it. So, get rid of the attraction of spreading harmful rumours by a media campaign that defuses rumour and becomes news in itself.
- Pay opinion leaders, if you have to, to discuss your side of the issues, but don't let the public know you paid them.
- Tell the whole world that you're going to bring lawsuits against all the rumour spreaders.

Source: Hendon 2001.

may build credibility and set positive trend for the product resulting in significant increase in sales.

In some E.Cs, it may be difficult to find a specialized PR agency: companies may then decide to avail of the help of their advertising agencies and their contacts with the local media. If there are specialized media buying agencies, they may certainly help in the handling of with the local media, thanks to their regular interaction with the same. Other times there may be individual professionals known to the company who may have good relationships with the media and could provide useful support.

Box 4.7 shows an effective use of PR to get the support of local politicians, who become in the specific case the brand ambassador in the launch of a new variant of an existing brand.

Box 4.7 HALLS VITA C ON THE GHANIAN MARKET

The Deputy Minister of Trade and Industry Mr Kwadwo Affram Asiedu has said that the Government would continue to create the right environment for private sector growth so that companies in Ghana can continue to expand their investments, businesses and create employment.

The Deputy Minister was speaking at the launch of Hall Vita C by Cadbury Ghana in Accra.

He said Cadbury has given support in the areas of quality water provision in the country and has provided over 300 wells over the years for various rural farming communities under the company's 'Ghana for the source' project.

He commended the company for the contribution in the fight against malaria, where staff and management participated in a project targeted at a million people and also for the purchase of mosquito nets for deprived communities in Ghana.

(Box 4.7—continued)

(*Box 4.7—continued*)

> Mr Affram said Halls Vita C is a fruit flavored candy with functional benefits such as providing preventive relief from colds and coughs and encouraged the company to add more value to Ghana's economy by sourcing locally. The raw materials in the company's manufacturing processes.
>
> The Commercial Director of the company Mr James Boateng said the introduction of Halls Vita C, is Cadbury's response to satisfying an unfulfilled Ghanian consumer need for a high quality fruity semi medicated brand.
>
> He said globally, Vita C belongs to the Halls family which is the biggest confectionery brand in the world, and the introduction to the Ghanian consumer would satisfy the quest for a high quality well differentiated brand.
>
> 'The brand is vitamin C enriched, very good testing, mildly mint and provides soothing preventative relief from cold and coughs'.

Source: Josephine Tsekpo. www.aacra-mail.com/mailnews.asp?id=15841
Posted on the Web on 9 March 2006.

Notes

1. These should be sent in good working condition and with adequate supply of spare parts, so as to avoid unnecessary production interruption in case of difficulties to find local provision of the same.
2. It is therefore advisable to build or procure a building which could accommodate also new lines in the future, thus over dimensioned versus the initial space requirement.
3. A 'push' strategy involves a push from the manufacturer through the intermediaries (own sales force or trade) to ensure that the products are made available to the end consumer; a 'pull' strategy aims to generate demand for the products directly at consumer level, normally through advertising, so as to pull the products through the intermediary chain.
4. This is still the case in India, for instance, at the moment when we write. However, the signal given by the government over

the last few months indicates an upcoming opening of the sector in the near future. A first step in this direction has been taken in 2006 by allowing foreign investors to detain some percentage of 'Single Brand' stores (see Box 4.5: FDI in Retail in India, Chapter 4, Section 4.2.5). On the other hand, China already has a well-developed modern trade, accounting for as much as 40 per cent of the total FMCG products sales (see Box 4.3: Wal-Mart Grows Bold in China).

5. Though there are marketing researches that try to measure the effect of the individual marketing variables on the sales, the results of these usually give indications rather than 'scientific evidences' of their effectiveness.

6. While it would be wrong to generalize, this is also one of the reasons why in E.M., coeteris paribus, employees show a much lower loyalty to a workplace and change job for a differential of few percentage points in their salaries.

7. Alternative methods are target return pricing, value-perceiving pricing and others.

8. It is a strategy where the investments to support a certain brand are minimized in order to maximize the contribution margin generated by the same; therefore, the brand becomes a 'cash cow' to be milked, as per the definition given by a renowned Boston Consulting Group matrix used to analyze the brand portfolio of a company at a given time.

9. S.E.C refers to the Socio-economic Clusters which are classified using the alphabet letters: cluster A represent the highest (the richest/most educated), B and following are lower clusters.

References

Hendon, D.W. 2001. *Classic Failures in Product Marketing*, Malaysia: Hardknocks Factory.

Kotler, P., S.H. Ang, S.M. Leong and C.T. Tan. 1999. *Marketing Management, An Asian Perspective*, Singapore: Prentice Hall.

Leonnet, J.P. and H.D. Hennessey. 1995. *Global Marketing Strategies*, Boston: Houghton Mifflin.

Levitt, T. 1983. 'The Globalization of Markets', *Harvard Business Review* (May–June).

Prahalad, C.K. and K. Lieberthal. 1998. 'The End of Corporate Liberalism', *Harvard Business Review*.

5

THE IMPORTANCE OF ETHICS

*Power drives to corruption and absolute power corrupts
beyond any redemption —J. Acton*

*It is odd, is it not, that a person's worth to society is measured
by his wealth, when instead his wealth should be measured
by his worth to society —A. Cygni*

5.1 Sustainable Development

There are a few challenges that the BRIC countries and more in general the E.Cs will have to
face during the coming decades.
Many of the projections quoted in the earlier
chapters are based on assumptions which could be
questionable but are built on economic models. Such
models use several variables and the actual data of
the past years to forecast some possible scenarios. One
of the mentioned assumptions is the sustainability
of the growth rate in the BRIC countries, which could
only be ensured if adequate policies and infrastructures

supporting the growth are put in place and maintained by the governments of the same. While the assumption of a sustainable growth seems to be happening, in reality when the total data of the BRIC countries are analysed for the years immediately successive to the Goldman Sachs' projections (2004 and 2005), there are some other variables normally not considered in the economic models which have the potential of completely changing the perspective not only in the E.Ms, but also more generally in the global scenario.

We shall mention some of these variables in order to have a more complete picture of the possible development of the E.Cs as well as their role in tomorrow's world.

The first important factor which comes to our scrutiny is the impact on the regional economies of the increased demand for commodities in the fast growing E.Cs. Some of the effects of this have already been experienced during 2004 and 2005, when the soaring demand for steel and oil from China and India had strongly contributed to a steep increase in the price of these commodities (see Figure 5.1).

Within 2030 China will have overtaken and India will be about to overtake the USA as the world's largest car markets: this will imply that their demand for steel and oil will dramatically increase, with conse-quences on price of the said materials and derivative, environment and possibly political stability. By that time the two countries together would probably account for more than 40 per cent of the global demand for oil: in a picture where the oil reserves are gradually being depleted, one could easily imagine the consequences of this. What is now a sound commercial competition among countries will then become a fierce battle

FIGURE 5.1 FORGING AHEAD

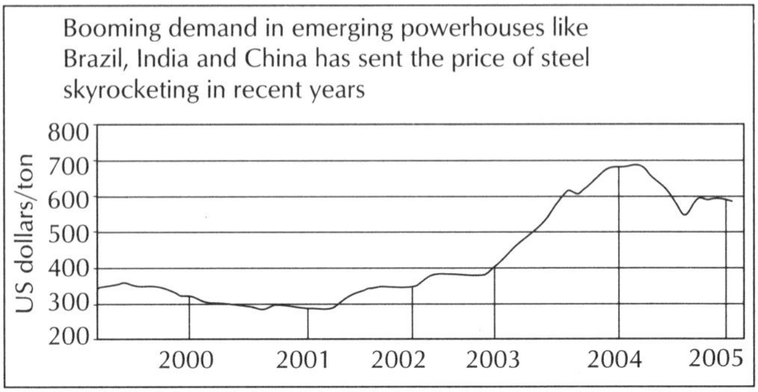
Booming demand in emerging powerhouses like Brazil, India and China has sent the price of steel skyrocketing in recent years
US dollars/ton
800
700
600
500
400
300
200
2000
2001
2002
2003
2004
2005

Source: Time, February 2006.

leading to an exponential increase of the market prices; the scarcity of indispensable resources could cause diplomatic tensions, which would ultimately increase the risk of a military conflict. Some preliminary signals of such tensions were experienced in a meeting which happened in New Delhi in November 2004, when India, China, South Korea and Japan, together with Russia and some other oil producers, met to discuss the idea of an Asian network of gas and energy. During the meeting both India and South Korea stated loudly that the age when their oil production was controlled by others was over and the Asian nations needed to plan how to autonomously manage their energy needs (see Figure 5.2).

Another more recent episode of growing tension around energy took place little over one year later, when, due to a dispute between Russia and Ukraine on the price of the gas supplied by the former to the latter, Russia partially stopped the supplies of it not only to Ukraine but also to some other European countries.

Related to this factor we should consider the heavy environmental impact of a steeply increased consumption of oil by the E.Cs: it is known that in most of

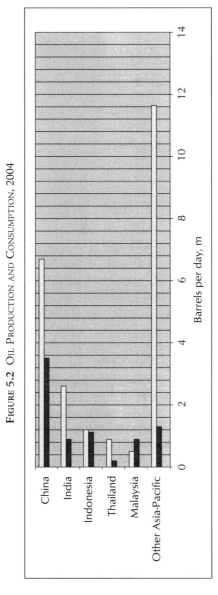

FIGURE 5.2 OIL PRODUCTION AND CONSUMPTION, 2004

Source: BP Statistical Review of World Energy.

them the usage of the same is highly inefficient as well as more polluting than in the developed countries. Therefore, the consequences of the exploitation of the underground world reserves together with the increased usage of more polluting machineries could have unpredictable consequences on the world's already challenged environmental balance. A scary anticipation of such a scenario happened as recently as in November 2005, when in the heart of China, in Jilin, a city on the banks of the Songhua River, an explosion in a petrochemical plant produced a massive cloud of toxic smoke. Initially, officials denied that the explosion had caused toxic air pollution and did not mention at all the possible water pollution. This was admitted only nine days after the event, one day after the officials of Harbin, a city which is 350 kilometres downriver from the plant, announced that they would shut off the city's water for reasons of pipe maintenance. Some more kilometres downstream the Songhua River flows across the Russia border in the Amu River, but China waited at least a week after the explosion to notify Russia about the toxins. The consequences of this incident are not yet known at the time when we are writing, but the way in which the whole case was handled gives a worrying signal of how future circumstances could negatively impact the world environment.

The heartening development that appeared in the Chinese press[1] in June 2006 is the disclosing of a 'white book on environmental protection' released by the Chinese Government. In this Beijing admits that the trade-off between economic development and environmental protection exists and needs to be seriously considered. In the book the commitments of the Government towards the defence of the environment are listed and clearly quantified (e.g., the major polluting discharges will need to be reduced by 10 per cent by 2010).

Hopefully these commitments will also be implemented and not only announced. The Chinese Government does not have very good records on transparency. As a matter of fact, the above mentioned pollution episode was not the first time that the Chinese authorities tried to cover up a disaster and eventually got caught. Similar circumstances had happened during the 2003 SARS crisis (see Box 5.1).

Box 5.1 CHINA LEARNS OF POLLUTANT PERILS
AS THE MERCURY RISES

'Beijing likes to vaunt its progress towards becoming a "green" city for the 2008 Olympics but it is more often a drab shade of grey... In recent years the emissions generated by China's breackneck industrialization have become more troublesome, not only for its neighbors but for faraway countries too. The most worrying export is airborne mercury, a dangerous neurotoxin spewed from coal-burning power and industrial plants...This contaminates fish and people eat fish. The effects are also seen in wildlife, where mercury accumulates in tissues... a mass contamination of Arctic wildlife... is making these animals less capable of surviving the harsh Arctic conditions and the impacts of climate change.

The Chinese government has said it is taking steps to reduce toxic emissions. Wen Jiabao, Prime Minister, recently ordered local governments to release detailed information on energy consumption and emissions every six months.

(Box 5.1—continued)

(*Box 5.1—continued*)

> He has also instructed top environment officials to deal with the extreme levels of China's pollution crisis. But... the country's State Environmental Protection Administration has limited staff and authority... and the government still lacks an effective system of incentives to persuade polluters to install emissions-control equipment while imposing serious fines on violators'.

Source: *Financial Times*, Asia, 13 July 2006.

This takes us to the second variable not always factored in the models of growth of the E.Ms, which is the spreading of pandemic events. History has taught that such disgraces are extremely difficult to foresee, thus often not taken into account; yet are responsible for major changes in the population of some countries and consequently on their development.

An example of this is what was called the Spanish Flu, which in the early twentieth century was responsible for the death of hundreds of thousands of people. At that moment, the scarcity of medications capable of fighting the disease was the main reason explaining the highest number of deaths recorded. On the other hand, at that time people were much less mobile than they are today, when the availability of thousands of daily international flights makes the transmissibility of a possible disease much easier and more difficult to control. This is being experienced at the outset of the twenty-first century, when cases of SARS, a respiratory disease, as well as bird flu, a sort of influenza virus transmitted through the contact with infected birds, are detected in several countries, far apart from each other. Such diseases and particularly the bird flu, have the potential to mutate into man to man transmissible ones, thus giving origin to pandemics which could cause millions of deaths with disastrous consequences on the world socio-economic scenario. However, mutations have not yet been detected, and the number of people killed by the mentioned diseases is still (officially) low.

Different is the situation as far as AIDS/HIV spreading is concerned, which is clearly an important challenge for most of the E.Cs. In 2004, 40 million cases of AIDS were recorded in the world; after Africa, the continent which has the highest number of infected people (25 million HIV-positive in the Sub-Saharan region only), India comes second with over 5 million cases estimated by UNAIDS in 2003. At the same time, the other BRIC countries were estimated at 0.9 (Russia), 0.8 (China) and 0.7 (Brazil). One could reasonably expect that these estimates are optimistic, given the scarce availability of data in most of these countries, as well as the high number of undeclared cases which go unrecorded.

Unfortunately, the forecasts[2] do not seem to paint an optimistic scenario, since by 2010 the number of infected cases could be as high as 20–25 million in India, 10–15 million in China and 5–8 million in Russia. This loss would thus, have the highest infected rate (3 to 6 per cent), (see Box 5.2) which would impact the already decreasing population causing as much as 0.5 per cent lower annual GDP growth from 2010, and up to 1 per cent lower growth from 2020 (Janson and Larsen 2004).

Box 5.2 SPREAD OF AIDS FORECAST TO CUT INDIA'S GROWTH

'The spread of HIV and Aids will knock almost a whole percentage point off India's average annual economic growth in the next decade, according to a United Nations-sponsored study... The report is the first detailed explanation of the growing impact of the disease on India... The epidemic could be pulling gross domestic product growth down by as much as 1.5 percentage points in 10 years' time, according to V.P. Rao, an NCAER economist. The loss of output would be most acute in sectors reliant on unskilled labor, such as tourism and manufacturing... Per capita annual income growth will fall by an average of 0.55 percentage point, to 6.13 per cent.'

Source: Financial Times, Asia, 21 July 2006.

The above numbers give an idea of the high potential impact on the macro-economic (and consequently also micro-economic) environment of pandemic health diseases, which most of the time are not factored in the countries' forecast, let alone in the companies' business plans.

A third important variable only recently partially considered at a macro level, but more and more influencing the investment decisions in an E.M. is the internal security of a country; more specifically the impact of terrorism on this. While the country risk provided by international bodies such as Dun & Bradstreet, Standard & Poor and the World Bank did include the internal stability in the different factors contributing to the final ranking of the country, before the twin towers attack on September 11 nobody could have anticipated the fast spreading of terrorism and the socio-economic impact of the same. In the more developed countries, an important percentage of resources in the annual financial budget have been diverted towards national security, thus in some way negatively affecting the resources which could have been dedicated to the cooperation and developmental activities in the E.Cs. Apart from the loss derived from the mentioned diversion, the impact of local terrorist attacks, such as those that happened in Bali in 2002 and 2005 or in Bangladesh in the latter half of 2005, on the economies of the countries is dramatic. The large reduction of tourism recorded in Bali during the months following the first of the mentioned attacks severely impacted the economy of the island, with non marginal negative influence on the entire country's GDP growth. The sequence of suicidal bomb blasts that rocked Bangladesh during the last quarter of 2005 is bound to have negative repercussions on the country's risk assessment and consequently on the level of incoming foreign direct investments.[3]

Even more worrying are the potential consequences of the socio-political impact that terrorism could imply. After the terrorist attack of July 2005 by British citizens of Islamic origin in the London underground tube, an even stronger anti-Islamic sentiment seems to be spreading across the world, from USA to Europe and across Asia to Oceania. On 12 December 2005, some unprecedented episodes of intolerance towards probable citizens of Middle East in Australia were filmed by the local television and aired through the international news channels. The violence shown was truly scary, and would certainly have left an impact in the minds of those who watched it. Such incidents can contribute to feed a dangerous inter-religious tension which may eventually generate a large scale social conflict or even war, possibly one of the most ferocious ever experienced.

In this section we have just touched upon three major themes with the potential to impact the world socio-economic scenario, and particularly the E.Ms. Though these variables as mentioned, are only partly factored in the macro-economic picture of the individual country, they need to be seriously considered while evaluating the investment in an E.M. Even once if the decision of entry has been taken and the company is already operating in these countries, factors like the environmental impact, the health risks or the terrorism threat must be a matter of regular thinking of the top management, since their relevance on the business results cannot be underestimated.

5.2 Red Tape, Corruption and Values

A cheap labour force for the manufacturers, a 'hungry consumer' for the marketers and a long-term young population are peculiarities of the ECs. The same are also responsible for some of the most painful hurdles a foreign investor is likely to face while operating in an emerging country: a heavy bureaucratic machine and a widely spread practice of corruption.

Many E.Cs have very limited fiscal revenues due to the low tax paying basis, sometimes as restricted as 5 per cent or less of the total population. On the other hand, we know in most of the E.Cs, due to a heavy presence of state companies and large administrative structures, public employment represents an important part of the total workforce. The consequence of this is that most of the public employees have very low salaries, many times below the level which could grant a comfortable standard of living. These same officers have sometimes large discretionary powers, which enable them to considerably slow down the already long and often complicated procedures that private companies need to complete in order to be able to obtain the initial approvals or the renewal of the licenses to operate. Given the circumstances, many of the public employees discover very early in their career how to use their discretionary power to gain easy money and improve their quality of life at the expense of the investors, the business people and even the ordinary man on the street.

Foreign investors often fall in the trap of not following all the (sometimes) obsolete prescribed regulations, thus becoming highly vulnerable to situations of harassment. In these circumstances, long delays in obtaining the necessary approvals and frustrating situations where the application procedures have to be started from scratch over and over again, can become a true nightmare. At times, even following scrupulously all the prescribed regulations does not save from such situations, since the interpretation of the same leaves enough space to find unnecessary faults sufficient to create hassles and delays.

Some practical examples will help understand how these loops are created (see Boxes 5.3–5.4).

Box 5.3 Red Tape in Brazil and Russia

BRAZIL

An MNC operating in the FMCG sector needed to open a warehouse from which the products stored would be invoiced and sent to their distributors.

The application to obtain the consent to operate the warehouse had to be approved by the municipality where it was

---

(Box 5.3—continued)

(Box 5.3—continued)

located. In the specific case, a very small village nearby the warehouse had only a few inhabitants. However, in the books of the Statistical Office of the same municipality there had not been previous cases of invoicing warehouses, thus there was no statistical code to be inserted in the books in order to allow the municipality to issue a license under that code. The matter was discussed in several offices and at different territorial levels, but apparently there was no solution that could be taken without the existence of the code.

After two years of unfruitful efforts, the Company decided to change the designation of the warehouse, so as to match the specifications of a code already existing in the statistical books.

RUSSIA

An MNC operating in the food sector decided to set up a manufacturing plant in Russia, where they had been operating for many years through importers with local sales and marketing activities.

Once the main guidelines of the projects had been decided, the land where the factory would be built selected and the drawing of the construction drafted, they started the process of applying to the local authorities for the necessary consent to purchase the land, building the factory and eventually commissioning the plant.

Since the initial steps took several months, they were advised to start the construction while waiting for the different consents, since this was the normal way of operating in Russia. However, after more than one year from the time the building works started, the company had not yet obtained the official document of possession of the land, since in the meantime it had been discovered to be part of some military territory to be used in case of emergency as national defense shelter. Despite this, the work was already at an advanced stage and stopping

(Box 5.3—continued)

(Box 5.3—continued)

them now would have implied a considerable loss of money: they therefore, decided to proceed anyway with it. After one more year the factory had almost been completed and the official property was finally obtained: the second stage was to apply for the ecological consent. During this process, the lay-out of the plant (almost completed now) had to be approved by the authorities before the consent for beginning the construction could be given. However the plant layout turned out to be non-compliant with the ecological specifications (though it had informally been previously approved), and the company was requested to modify it, which would of course imply a large investment at this stage. The ecological phase went on for over one year and in the meantime the factory was actually completed, whereas it did not officially exist yet.

The overall process of obtaining the licenses lasted for over four years and the factory, with already installed lines and people hired, could not operate, despite having been completed for over one year. In the meantime, the Company accumulated a large amount of financial losses and cash flow problems due to the immobilized and unutilized investment.

Box 5.4 Corruption in Russia

During the initial years of the new century, a Swiss Company in the amusement park sector that did not see much growth in its home market started seeking business opportunities in the emerging countries. They explored the Russian market also and decided to set up a joint venture for two operations in Moscow with a Russian Company. Normally in similar ventures the local partner takes care of the logistics of the machineries as well as of the visas of the expatriates who would come to start up and run the same.

(Box 5.4—continued)

(*Box 5.4—continued*)

The first operation ran smoothly, but the second one had results much below expectations, also due to the unexpected bad weather. The local partner, who had been the cause of the mentioned delays, started complaining about the financial losses and wanted to find a way to make up for them. He proposed delaying the foreseen re-export of the equipment, in view of a possible new operation, which however, never materialized. Eventually, the re-export deadline expired, and, as per the local law, the company could be liable to pay a customs fee up to 100 per cent of the machines value in order to re-export them beyond the authorized deadline. The foreign partner did not want to pay such large amount and a litigation with the local partner started. As this became more acute, pressures from lawyers and later even physical threats for the employees of the foreign company started. In the meantime the demurrage expenses for the equipment withheld in the customs' warehouses were increasing. Also, a new interpretation of the export–import laws stated that if at least two-thirds of the value of the equipment in contention was not deposited within a certain deadline, the custom authorities were entitled to start an auction and keep the proceedings of the same as compensation for the demurrage and other expenses incurred. As time passed, the visas for the expatriates expired and they were running the risk of violating the immigration laws with severe consequences. It was finally understood that a payment was expected by some official. It was suggested through intermediaries that this be done in an off-shore account through which the money could eventually come back to the concerned people.

Subsequently, it was realized that such cases were rather common and the vague clause in the import–export law which would start a similar mechanism was being often interpreted against the foreign companies to cause the planned consequences.

In the worst cases, the mala fide of the shrewd bureaucrat gets to the point of purposely creating the fault in order to be able to propose his service to 'oblige' the counterpart. The pressures become particularly effective when the necessary approval can dramatically delay the start of an important operation, thus creating considerable loss of revenues. At times threat of criminal procedures against the apex of the companies are used with similar objectives, a particularly effective way of harassing when the directors of the same are non-resident foreign people: if the procedure was to be initiated they would need to fly to the concerned country to appear before the court and request the bail. Rather than facing such circumstances, the local management obviously prefers to pay some goodwill fee which will keep at bay the appetite of the concerned officer, at least till the next time such a transaction happens. And once the willingness of the 'criminal' company to settle the issue in a smoother way is ascertained, the next occasion will not be delayed too long and will possibly imply an even more serious, thus more expensive violation.

How to avoid such unfortunate situations? The first golden rule might seem obvious, but is often forgotten: scrupulously observe laws and make sure that no violation is detectable. Whenever the company is clearly caught on the wrong side, the threats become much stronger and the possible way out could become extremely expensive. However, in some E.Cs literally following the local laws and regulations could mean to put a halt to the operations, or at least to incur significant difficulties which could cause unnecessary costs or loss of opportunities.

In such cases, the management could decide to take a measured risk and find a wise way to operate with border line practices, which are not illegal, but might be interpreted as such, depending on how strictly the law is considered. Whenever such risks are taken, the company will have to ensure that all possible objections which could be raised have already been studied with the appropriate consultants and in case the matter is contested and brought to court, there are reasonable possibilities to fight the argument.

According to the risk orientation of the management, such decisions could happen more or less frequently: the balance between risk and opportunity is normally found after some years of operation and acquired knowledge of the local authorities and their way of acting. Our suggestion is however to limit such risks to the strictly indispensable circumstances, when the company's business would be seriously compromised unless a solution is found to the difficulty/impediment created by the newly introduced regulation.

Apart from hurdles created by cunning officers, it is not rare to find that the temptations of easy money have won the resistance of some employees. The departments where similar incidents may occur more often are those with direct contact with external partners, therefore, Purchasing, Accounting, Sales and HR. The strategies used by those who want to obtain favours (normally getting business) from the employees in the mentioned departments (or in other departments) start with testing the potential 'facilitators' with gifts and personal invitations, and progressively increase the value of the former or the attractiveness of the latter (from an invitation to a lunch, to a free weekend, to a whole paid holiday). The creation of the personal rapport with the employee normally ensures that the same provides at least a preferential treatment to the partner; sometimes the relationship goes much further, and the employee gets in collusion with the supplier and shares in return part of the benefits enjoyed by this.

While there is not, in our knowledge and experience, a 100 per cent foolproof remedy to this risk, there are a few actions which, when adequately implemented, can help reduce the occurrence of such incidents.

a) The first and the most important is the creation and spreading of a few clear value anchors, which should function as a guide to the individuals in their day-to-day work. These values should be circulated throughout the organization and discussed at all levels: each employee should have a thorough knowledge and understanding of their meaning; his performances should also be appraised vis-à-vis the values and the company culture and various activities should be built around them.

b) Based on the values, a code of conduct should be created and circulated. In this, a clear articulation of the expected way of reacting to specific situations, with examples of the most frequent difficult decisions or dilemmas one might face, should complement the statement of principles derived from the values and the best practices.

c) Policies, job descriptions, letters of authority and other internal procedures and documents should fix clear guidelines for the expected behaviour of the employees and should regularly be updated and discussed with them. The objective is to limit as much as possible the grey areas and the discretional choice, particularly in case of ethical dilemmas.

d) Apart from the written documentation, the best way to create a culture based on ethics is to lead by examples and 'walk the talk'. The behaviour of the top management will be the benchmark for the rest of the organization and the integrity of the management team should not leave space for any possible doubt.

Additional sound practices such as job rotation, inter-department transfers and internal audit will certainly help.

Last but not the least, observing the behaviour and personal habits of employees outside the work hours could also provide useful indications about possible problems. A standard of life disproportionate to the salary paid to an individual might lead the management to think that additional sources of income have been found by the same.

In conclusion, ethical behaviour is particularly important while doing business in an E.M. (see Table 5.1) Individuals normally grow up in an environment where 'shortcuts' and corruption are widely spread and accepted as normal practices: making sure that this frame of mind is radically changed while operating in a company requires a continuous effort, the results of which are not always successful.

5.3 Corporate Social Responsibility (CSR)

Operating in an E.C. is a source of revenue for the companies, employment for local resources, tax income for the local governments and immense knowledge for

TABLE 5.1 INDEX OF CORRUPTION PERCEPTION

	Score CPI 2004
Finland	9.7
New Zealand	9.6
Denmark	9.5
Iceland	9.5
Singapore	9.3
Sweden	9.2
Switzerland	9.1
Norway	8.9
Australia	8.8
Netherlands	8.7
United Kingdom	8.6
Canada	8.5
Austria	8.4
Luxembourg	8.4
Germany	8.2
Hong Kong	8.0
Belgium	7.5
Ireland	7.5
USA	7.5
Chile	7.4
France	7.1
Spain	7.1
Japan	6.9
Israel	6.4
Portugal	6.3
Uruguay	6.2
Botswana	6.0
Estonia	6.0
Slovenia	6.0
Taiwan	5.6
Jordan	5.3
Malaysia	5.0
Tunisia	5.0

(Table 5.1—continued)

(*Table 5.1—continued*)

	Score CPI 2004
Costa Rica	4.9
Hungary	4.8
Italy	4.8
Lithuania	4.6
South Africa	4.6
South Korea	4.5
Trinidad and Tobago	4.2
Bulgaria	4.1
Mauritius	4.1
Namibia	4.1
Brazil	3.9
Peru	3.5
Poland	3.5
China	3.4
Belarus	3.3
Jamaica	3.3
Dominican Republic	2.9
India	2.8
Russia	2.8
Tanzania	2.8
Ethiopia	2.3
Honduras	2.3
Zimbabwe	2.3
Cote D'iviore	2.0
Nigeria	1.6
Bangladesh	1.5

Source: www.transparency.org

Note: Scores vary from 1 to 10, the highest being equivalent to a more transparent and less corrupt environment.

the expatriates, or in general the foreign managers who will be exposed to a completely different working and living experience in these markets.

When companies achieve the return on their investments and start generating the planned profits, they normally reinvest part of the same in order to enhance their growth and consolidate their market share. While this process sometimes takes longer than foreseen,[4] once profits start to happen it is wise to reinvest at least a minimal part of them in activities of social responsibilities. Corporate Social Responsibility (CSR) can be defined as 'a company's obligation to be reasonable to all of its stakeholders... with the aim of achieving sustainable development ... also in the social and environmental dimension.'[5]

Reflecting on Peter Drucker's (2003) considerations on the three needs of a healthy society (effective government, business and community organizations), one would soon realize that in an E.C. the effectiveness of the public sector is not controllable by the private investors and is normally quite low. This clearly impacts on the community organizations' effectiveness, which therefore need the support of the private sector to counterbalance the inadequacy of the public one.

In most of the E.Cs the opportunities to be involved in such activities will be numerous at any point of time of the development of the business, since large pockets of poverty as well as poor health, education and infrastructure are so evident that one does not really need to go and search for them. The suggestion to start these activities once a threshold of profitability is achieved is given for two basic reasons. The first is that, during the first years of operation, the attention of all resources will be fully dedicated to the business in the effort to maximize the return on the investment in the shortest time possible. Consequently, there will not be much time left to evaluate and implement similar activities, which could be to some extent defocusing for some of the resources. For the same reasons, most of the financial resources available will be used for the ordinary business, and the possible need of funds for the working capital would not leave much space for extra investments. The second reason is in some way an effect of the first: once the structure is in place, the revenues start flowing and so do the profits, there would be more funds available and the company would start paying taxes. Since most of social activities are recognized as expenses deductible from the corporate income tax, the company will have the double benefit of achieving their social objectives while saving on taxes, thus the same activities would actually become even more affordable.

The aim of giving back to the society a part of what the company earns from it is a noble and respected principle for any institution, business partner or righteous individual. While acting as a good corporate citizen a company gains credibility and reinforces its image vis-à-vis the local authorities and at the same time obtains mileage which could be spent at the appropriate moment. Examples are the activities undertaken by companies with manufacturing facilities for the benefit of the people living in the villages or towns in the proximity of the same. Specifically in the E.Cs while helping the closeby villages to improve the local infrastructure, for instance, donating the necessary funds to build a stretch of road, or to bring the electric power to another neighbourhood, the company will increase the goodwill of the society, gain visibility and good reputation and at the same time increase its negotiating power in case of possible future problems. If ever some matters come up for discussion due to a mistake of an employee or other unforeseen circumstances, the local authorities, as well as some individuals who might have been affected by the matter, will most likely be ready to be more forgiving and settle the issue in an amicable way.

If the social activities undertaken happen to be in education (building or renovating schools, etc.) and contacts are established with the students, the company will find in those benefited some possible brand ambassadors who would carry in their mind for a good part of their life the positive image of the benefits received and could become loyal consumers of the company's goods or services.

The bigger the size of business, the higher will be the expectation from the local institutions to see an active involvement of the foreign company in social responsibility activities (see Box 5.5).

BOX 5.5 RETHINKING THE CONCEPT OF CSR

...Corporate philanthropy can never be enough to address the environmental and social emergencies that confront us. Avoiding pollution, adopting the community's school, carrying out immunization programs (...) must continue, but they are like re-arranging the deck chairs on the Titanic while the ship is sailing towards imminent disaster (...). CSR must be directed towards two objectives. One is to reduce corporation's net consumption of natural resources to zero and thereafter to add back resources to the environment. The other is to create a pattern of economic activity by which poor people in the communities and countries in which the corporations operate can see a direct connection between the growth of the corporation's activities and profit and their own incomes (...). Philanthropy can at best deploy only a fraction of the profits of the corporations to do good, whereas it is the main business activity of the corporation to which attention must be urgently directed. This is because it may be the core business model and business processes that, albeit indirectly and inadvertently, create the very conditions in society that make such philanthropy

---

(Box 5.5—continued)

(*Box 5.5—continued*)

> necessary. The role of corporations cannot be limited only to producing financial value for financial investors. It must encompass the production of value more broadly defined and from the perspective of many stakeholders within which financial value for financial investors is an essential component no doubt. Clearly we cannot expect CSR managers to rethink the core purpose of the corporation and its central business model. This is the job of the CEO and the Board. Therefore, only when we see CEOs and not CSR managers at the CSR meetings (...) we will begin to address the deep conceptual crisis in CSR.

Source: The *Financial Express*, Mumbai, 22 January 2006.

Global players do not have the choice of not supporting the local communities. On the other hand, their CSR activities are often a good shelter to counter balance the allegations sometimes raised by the anti-globalization organizations that are very prompt to use any possible means and manner to attack them. Even before the anti-American wave was experienced in several countries as a consequence of the Afghanistan and Iraq wars in early 2000, several cases of legal and sometimes even physical attacks to the large global companies took place during the nineties, when a strong anti-globalization movement spread over many Western countries. Brands like McDonald, Coca-Cola, Nike, Nestlé, were targets of loud boycott campaigns which went to the extent of inciting consumers not to purchase their products by advertising messages circulated through the net, thus provoking important losses of revenues.

Sometimes such attacks were caused by the discovery of malpractices actually happening in some of the E.Ms (sweatshops, child labour, etc.); but most of the time they had originated from a badly handled local incident, which had been amplified also due to the suboptimal relationship of the concerned company with the local associations, unions, institutions, media and consumers.

Effective antidotes to these possible risks are clearly the full compliance to the local law and regulations, the use of international best practices and codes of conduct while operating in an E.M., as well as sound PR and CSR activities.

It is recommended that companies operating in an E.M. make an effort to involve their employees in such initiatives stimulating the active participation of the individuals in such efforts, so as not to limit the scope of their social support to financial aid to local bodies or NGOs. This will yield a multiplying effect to the extent of the activities implemented, as well as provide the opportunity of an informal interaction among employees and a better understanding of the same.

The response obtained to such initiatives is likely to be more enthusiastic than that possibly obtained in developed countries. While it would be wrong to generalize, such a finding is possibly explained by the fact that the sense of solidarity seems to be stronger in people who live in more difficult conditions, such as those experienced in the E.Cs, rather than people living in more comfortable ones, as often is the case in developed countries.

If the CSR activities happen through local NGOs, and this could be the right choice particularly at the beginning, an accurate selection of the same prevent the misuse or optimal exploitation of the allocated resources. The association with the NGO selected will bring knowledge and networking capabilities to the

Box 5.6 THE ULTIMATE OBJECTIVE OF CSR

Companies allocate funds in CSR driven by the beliefs of their top management or shareholders, who decide to take up the philanthropy route for several reasons. Sometimes they are inspired by a genuine feeling of sharing part of their welfare with the society from where they have come up; some other time the thought of leaving a mark, being remembered is what pushes them to donate; other times the reasons are not only humanitarian, but also linked to other incentives (e.g., fiscal facilitations). Often it is not easy to justify such activities from a merely financial perspective: one would need to look at the bigger picture and think on the line of long term strategic benefits that could derive from them. For instance, the involvement of the employees in CSR activities could result in a motivational bond with the company, thus helping in the retention of talent. It becomes however more difficult to sustain long term social development program when the pressure from the 'non-inspired' shareholders for returns and profitability increases. Even in this case, activities reinforcing the company's core strategy may still find the approval of the boards. Examples of this are actions implemented by companies in emerging countries in order to improve the infrastructure necessary to run their business, yet providing benefits also to the local communities who can utilize the upgraded facilities. Companies like Nestlé, for example, have invested in what they call 'milk-production systems', by training farmers and enhancing their milk production skills, as well as creating a collection system and the related infrastructure that ensure a reliable supply for the company that packs and distributes the product. Similarly Coca-Cola has invested in improving the quality of the water supply of some villages in India: the purpose was linked to the fact that they use a large quantity of water, thus partly depleting the available supply for the villages in the proximity of their bottling plants.

(Box 5.6—continued)

(Box 5.6—continued)

In other circumstances, companies may try to create 'cause-related government relations', with the objective of getting favorable treatment in the future. Some firms in China have committed to help the government with its AIDS strategy:[6] their side objective may have been not only humanitarian.

Other firms believe that by running their business they are already creating wealth and benefiting the surrounding environment. Those who work for them will increase their consumptions and generate further wealth. This is certainly one way of looking at the issue, though not in the direction of 'exceeding the ethical, legal, commercial and public expectations that society has for business', that is said to be the ultimate goal of Corporate Social Responsibility.

The recent commitment of the richest man in the world, Bill Gates, to step down from his company's number one seat to devote time to the foundation created by him is by all means a major development in the corporate world. With his funds and his skills he will certainly benefit thousands of people in need and possibly trigger a wave of donations from those who have confidence in his capability and intentions. The wave has already started: another philanthropist has, soon after Gates' announcement, pledged a huge contribution to the Melinda and Bill Gates foundation, possibly the largest amount ever donated for these purposes: thirty seven billion dollars.

If this is only the start, there are hopes that the world will soon become a better place to live.

activities defined by the company: they (the NGOs) will provide a person who will act as an interface with the community to be benefited, since she would normally have a good personal rapport with the same. At a later stage, the company may decide to handle the activities through in-house resources: while this would require a larger involvement, it would certainly improve the span of control on the resources invested as well as create a closer bonding with the beneficiaries.

CSR activities are becoming more and more frequent among companies, particularly those of sizeable dimensions. In E.Ms the management realizes that the development of the community where they operate is a pre-condition for the long-term growth of the company they head.

While this is very positive and encouraging, companies who decide to get involved in these activities should remember that a real contribution to the society will happen only when this is enabled to have its own sustainable development. The empowerment of people through providing them the capability of developing their own instruments of income should be the ultimate objective of a responsible corporate.

Notes

1. See *People's Daily* (Beijing).
2. National Intelligence Council on CIA website.
3. Let us also consider that the E.Ms are an easy target of terrorist attacks: the limited national security budgets, as well as the lack of technology and the wide spread corruption make the organization of such an attack relatively simple.
4. We shall never be tired to recommend a large dose of patience while entering an E.M.
5. See www.timesfoundation.com
6. See *Economist*, 25 February 2006.

References

Drucker, Peter Ferdinand. 2003. *A Functioning Society: Selections from Sixty-Five Years of Writing on Community, Society, and Polity* London: Transaction Publishers.

Janson, T.M. and J.A.R. Larsen. 2004. 'The BRIC Countries', *Denmark's National Bank Monetary Review*, 4th Quarter.

6

EMERGING GLOBAL CHALLENGERS

*There is one thing stronger than all the armies in the world,
and that is an idea whose time has come —V. Hugo*

6.1 The Emerging Companies

Failure to prepare is preparing to fail —B. Franklin

For the last few years the magazine *BusinessWeek* has been publishing, based on a research done by Interbrand, the list of the 100 Top Global Brands by value.[1]

By looking at the evolution of the ranking during the years, one would realize that, while in the past the global brands were mainly in the FMCG sector, after the boom of the New Economy of the last decade of the twentieth century, technology brands such as Nokia and Microsoft have achieved position among the top ten (Pelle 2004). Also, while still in the 2005 list most of the brands' country of origin is America, a few (non-Japanese) Asian brands have started appearing in the same: new entry as Hyundai and LG have reached the lower part of the ranking, but others such as Samsung are climbing the ladder. This brand has now reached the twentieth position, and has been constantly going up in the rank for the last five years. In fact, two of the five brands that have reported the biggest gains in value in 2005 are from Asia,[2] and the single highest gainer is the Korean Samsung. It is quite interesting to recall that less than a decade ago the same company was the maker of low-end consumer electronics under different brand names, and this few market observers would have foreseen the success experienced in the subsequent years. The same *BusinessWeek* magazine also publishes the ranking of the 500 world's largest multinational companies: in the 2005 edition some 18 new Chinese companies have made it to the list, while some other European ones have made an exit (Rampini 2006).

The reality is that with the rapid growth of the E.Cs, some of the companies based in these have started their global expansion and are quickly gaining shares in several markets, both emerging but also developed ones. Some of them have chosen to attack the countries adjacent to their country of origin where they have the main business platform, so as to leverage on possible cultural similarities and business contacts (see Table 6.1). Some others are expanding directly in large developed markets: among these the Chinese and Indian companies are the ones that are focusing their efforts mainly towards the developed world (for India see Box 6.1).

The common traits of these players are thus the mentioned success in the domestic market and the growing financial muscles, the flexibility of their operations and the strong determination to repeat their home success story in other markets. Their competitive edge vis-à-vis the established multinational companies are the low cost advantage, deriving from the cheaper material and

TABLE 6.1 THE RDE 100 SPAN MULTIPLE INDUSTRIES AND COUNTRIES

Company	Industry	Country
Aluminum Corporation of China (Chalco)	Nonferrous Metals	China
America Movil	Telecommunication Services	Mexico
Bajaj Auto	Automotive Equipment	India
Bharat Forge	Automotive Equipment	India
BOE Hydis Technology Co.	Computers and IT Components	China
Braskem	Petrochemicals	Brazil
BYD Company	Consumer Electronics	China
Cemex	Building Materials	Mexico
Charoen Pokphand Foods	Food and Beverages	Thailand
China Aviation Corporation	Aerospace	China
China FAW Group Corporation	Automotive Equipment	China
China HuaNeng Group	Fossil Fuels	China
China International Marine Containers Group Company (CIMC)	Shipping	China
China Minmetals Corporation	Nonferrous Metals	China
China Mobile Communications Corporation	Telecommunications Services	China
China National Heavy Duty Truck Group Corporation (CNHTC)	Automotive Equipment	China
China Netcom Group Corporation (CNC)	Telecommunications Services	China
China Petroleum & Chemical Corporation (Sinopec)	Fossil Fuels	China
China Shipping Group	Shipping	China
Chunlan Group Corporation	Home Appliances	China

(Table 6.1—continued)

(Table 6.1—continued)

Company	Industry	Country
Cipla	Pharmaceuticals	India
CNOOC	Fossil Fuels	China
Companhia Vale do Rio Doce (CVRD)	Mining	Brazil
COSCO Group	Shipping	China
Coteminas	Textiles	Brazil
Crompton Greaves	Engineered Products	India
Dongfeng Motor Company	Automotive Equipment	China
Dr. Reddy's Laboratories	Pharmaceuticals	India
Embraco	Engineered Products	Brazil
Embraer	Aerospace	Brazil
Erdos Group	Textiles	China
Femsa	Food and Beverages	Mexico
Founder Group	Computers and IT Components	China
Galanz Group Company	Home Appliances	China
Gazprom	Fossil Fuels	Russia
Gerdau Steel	Steel	Brazil
Gree Electric Appliances	Home Appliances	China
Gruma	Food and Beverages	Mexico
Grupo Modelo	Food and Beverages	Mexico
Haier Company	Home Appliances	China
Hindalco Industries	Nonferrous Metals	India
Hisense	Consumer Electronics	China
Huawei Technologies Company	Telecommunication Equipment	China
Indofood Sukses Makmur	Food and Beverages	Indonesia
Infosys Technologies	IT Services/Business Process Outsourcing	India
Jonson Electric	Engineered Products	China/HK
Koc Holding	Home Appliances	Turkey
Konka Group Company	Consumer Electronics	China
Larsen & Toubro	Engineering Services	India
Lukoil	Fossil Fuels	Russia
Mahindra & Mahindra	Automotive Equipment	India

(Table 6.1—continued)

(*Table 6.1—continued*)

Company	Industry	Country
Malaysia International Shipping Co. (MISC)	Shipping	Malaysia
Midea Holding Co.	Home Appliances	China
MMC Norilsk Nickel Group	Nonferrous Metals	Russia
Mobile Telesystems (MTS)	Telecommunication Services	Russia
Nanjing Automobile Group Corporation (NAC)	Automotive Equipment	China
Natura	Cosmetics	Brazil
Nemak	Automotive Equipment	Mexico
Oil and Natural Gas Corporation (ONGC)	Fossil Fuels	India
Orascom Telecom Holding	Telecommunications Services	Egypt
Pearl River Piano Group	Musical Instruments	China
Perdigao	Food and Beverages	Brazil
PetroChina Company	Fossil Fuels	China
Petrobras	Fossil Fuels	Brazil
Petronas	Fossil Fuels	Malaysia
Ranbaxy Pharmaceuticals	Pharmaceuticals	India
Reliance Group	Chemicals	India
Rusal	Nonferrous Metals	Russia
Sabanci Holding	Chemicals	Turkey
Sadia	Food and Beverages	Brazil
Satyam Computer Services	IT Services/Business Process Outsourcing	India
Severstal	Steel	Russia
Shanghai Automotive Industry Corporation Group (SAIC)	Automotive Equipment	China
Shanghai Baosteel Group Corporation	Steel	China
Shougang Group	Steel	China
Sinochem Corporation	Chemicals	China
Sisecam	Building Materials	Turkey

(*Table 6.1—continued*)

(*Table 6.1—continued*)

Company	Industry	Country
Skyworth Multimedia International Company	Consumer Electronics	China
Sukhoi Company	Aerospace	Russia
SVA Group Company	Consumer Electronics	China
Tata Consultancy Services (TCS)	IT Services/Business Process Outsourcing	India
Tata Motors	Automotive Equipment	India
Tata Steel	Steel	India
Tata Tea	Food and Beverages	India
TCL Corporation	Consumer Electronics	China
Techtronic Industries Company	Engineered Products	China/HK
Thai Union Frozen Products	Food and Beverages	Thailand
Tsingtao Brewery	Food and Beverages	China
TVS Motor Company	Automotive Equipment	India
UTStarcom	Telecommunications Equipment	China
Vestel Group	Consumer Electronics	Turkey
Videocon Industries	Consumer Electronics	India
Videsh Sanchar Nigam (VSNL)	Telecommunication Services	India
Votorantim Group	Process Industries	Brazil
Wanxiang Group Corporation	Automotive Equipment	China
WEG	Engineered Products	Brazil
Wipro	IT Services/Business Process Outsourcing	India
ZTE Corporation	Telecommunication Equipment	China

Source: BCG Rapidly Developing Economies Analysis, May 2006.

labour cost available in their home country, the rapid learning process they are able to achieve, the possibility of selecting the best talent among a huge pool available in their (often) largely populated countries of origin and the willingness to work and live abroad of their resources. Even the most potential resources among the local ones posted in foreign countries would have a cost significantly lower than comparable resources in developed countries. In some of their home countries they avail of government incentives and subsidies; they also enjoy comparatively longer working weeks, thus a higher productivity, which make their products even more competitive versus the Western competitors. Added to these advantages is also the lower cost of the investments and utilities in their home country, since machineries are usually cheaper there and so is the cost of power and water. Also, most of these companies have already experienced the competition of the MNCs in their domestic markets and have learnt how to compete with them; they have gained a valuable know-how while operating in the difficult environment of the E.Cs, where it is harder to achieve profitable results, given the high price sensitivity of the local consumers. They are, therefore, able to offer reasonably priced products with growing quality levels.

These companies operate in different sectors: among the 100 mentioned (see Table 6.1), the largest number is in industrial goods, followed by consumer durables, and also food and cosmetics. Some of them have been early movers and had started the process of globalization during the last years of the past century; some others are making rapid progress in the process during the last two years; the rest have just started their internationalization and are today more regional than global. Their models of globalization are different. Some of them leverage on their engineering and research strength to provide services to third party: this is the case of Wipro, an

Indian IT group with a turnover of over two billion USD, which claims to be already the world's largest third-party provider of R&D services (Aguaiar et al. 2006). Others have specialized in a specific category and are competing globally in the same: Johnson Electric, a Hong Kong based company, produces small electric motors for automotive and other applications and has manufacturing facilities in Europe, United States and Middle East, other than China and Japan. Some of the companies leverage the abundance of natural resources in their home countries (e.g., the Brazilian Sadia); at the other extreme some others need to find natural resources in foreign countries (e.g., steel for Chinese companies), thus they establish ventures with companies in countries rich with the materials that they need.

In the steel industry, the Mittal Group, owned by the Indian Lakshmi Mittal, an entrepreneur who started the international expansion in 1994, has created an empire through international acquisitions. The Group bought companies in Kazakhstan, China, Mexico and some other African and Asian countries. Later it started moving its focus to European companies, in the Balkans and in other East European countries. In 2004 it took over the giant American International Steel Group for USD 4.5 billion, becoming one of the largest world producers of steel. In 2006 the company attempted a hostile takeover of the Luxemburg Arcelor. After several months of dispute and revisions of the initial bid, the acquisition was eventually finalized and the Mittal Group absorbed the European firm, enhancing its position in the world steel industry. The episode has been perceived in France and Luxembourg as a premonition of a scary future when the Asian players will progressively conquer and colonize Europe. The Mittal-Arcelor is not an isolated case. More and more emerging players are sealing deals with European partners: this is the case of the Indian Tata Group, a large diversified 18 USD billion group that signed a partnership with the Italian car producer Fiat in 2005. The number of M&A activities of the 100 companies shown in Table 6.1 is increasing every year: in 2005, only 59 acquisitions happened, versus the 15 in the year 2000 (Aguaiar et al. 2006).

All of these emerging companies have global ambitions and are investing in this direction. They are, in fact, working on their weak areas, such as innovation and long-term strategic planning, and are trying to get on board expatriates from other countries, so as to form capable and international management teams.

The current multinational companies will have to find the way to cope with the competition of their emerging counterparts, who are now coming to fight for the share in what used to be their own turf. They might want to face them head-on and leverage their current strengths to create higher entry barriers. They may do this through new unique marketing positioning or through higher R&D investments by creating more sophisticated technologies, sometimes abandoning products or industries where they are no more capable to compete. They might try to fight the incumbent companies also in their countries of origin, so as to weaken their main source of profitability and limiting their possibility of financing the investments abroad. Sometimes they may like to establish joint ventures with them, as in the cases mentioned earlier. Certainly they cannot afford ignoring them, with the risk of realizing too late, how potentially dangerous they are and ending up facing a take-over by them.

Box 6.1 INDIA'S GLOBAL ASSETS

(...) Though globalization of Indian companies existed ever since independence, the phenomenon gained momentum only in 2000. Thus, as the widespread attitude among Indian companies, globalization is still in its early days.

...The inorganic route has been the more preferred mode by Indian companies than the Greenfield or organic route for extending their global reach. The trendsetter for acquisitions was Tata Tea, whose takeover of Tetley Tea in 2000 was commendable considering that the acquirer was less than half the size of Tetley at the time of acquisition. The acquisition made Tata Tea the second largest tea company in the world. In late 2000, Essel Packaging, a domestic leader in laminated packaging tubes, took over Propack of Switzerland, thus becoming the largest laminating packaging company in the world. Some notable examples of organic growth have been the Tata Group, Mahindra & Mahindra and Sundaram Fasteners who have set up manufacturing facilities on foreign soil.

...According to statistics released by the Ministry of Finance, between April 01 and December 05, Indian overseas investment outflow amounted to USD 8 billion. Already USD 2.1 billion has been invested between Jan–Mar 06, thus taking the total acquisitions for FY06 close to USD 3 billion.

In terms of geographical spread, majority of the acquisitions have been in Europe and the US. (...) Acquisition of international oil and gas equity has been the single most compelling factor responsible for the outflow of foreign funds. Since 2000, of the total Indian overseas investment of USD 10 billion, investment made by ONGC Videsh Ltd. (OVL) alone amounted to USD 5 billion in acquiring oil and gas equity in 10 countries including Russia, Brazil, Sudan, Myanmar, Syria, Iraq, Iran, Libya, Vietnam and Angola. Apart from OVL, consortium of Indian Oil Corporation and Oil India Ltd. are also in talks for acquiring oil equity in Africa, and have earmarked at least USD 2–3 billion.

(Box 6.1—continued)

(Box 6.1—continued)

> The manufacturing sector acquisitions are mainly of small firms with the average size of acquisition estimated at USD 30 million. The largest acquisition in value terms in the manufacturing sector was Dr Reddy's takeover of Betapharm in Germany for USD 570 million. There exists a huge market for Indian services abroad and mergers and acquisitions would be the most logical extension for formalizing this demand. A few niche non-traditional industries that would be bellwethers of globalization are media, consultancy, research and development, educational services. International support to Indian services is also evident from the widespread business process outsourcing that is currently taking place. While most of the operations are being carried out on Indian soil, there could be a trend wherein Indian expertise in the service sector area is transported as corporate entities abroad.

Source: Dun & Bradstreet on 'India in Perspective', May 2006.

6.2 A New Geopolitical Scenario

Like it cannot happen that in the Sky there are two Suns, so it cannot be that on Earth there are two emperors —**Confucio**

6.2.1 Asia on the Rise

The development of the economy of a country is closely linked to the evolution of its political situation, both internal and external. It is not by chance that most of the E.Cs have started growing at the rates we are now seeing after they have achieved a relatively stable internal socio-political situation and have opened their markets to international trade and investors.

In this and the following sections, we shall briefly try to analyse the global geopolitical scenario, with a closer focus on what is now happening in Asia, where two of the most potential E.Cs, China and India, are now changing the world economic and political power equilibrium.

Going back to only two decades, two superpowers used to dominate the geopolitical world scenario, USA and USSR. This situation had evolved from a Eurocentric model of the nineteenth century, when the main European Nations, England, France and Germany, had divided their spheres of influences in the Vienna Conference of 1815 and used to rule the scene. The rise of USA and Russia happened in the twentieth century and specifically after the World Wars, which marked the defeat of Germany and Japan, the two challengers who had tried to flex their muscles through expansionist campaigns even before the culmination of the Second World War.

If we look at the world in a wide geopolitical perspective, we may divide it into three main blocks: the American, the European and the Asian. These correspond to some extent to the continents, with the exception that so far the African has had too many internal problems to have a strong say in the world panorama and Australia's size is far too small to significantly influence the rest of the players.

We may then say that during the second half of the twentieth century, the two main dominating poles of attraction were USA and USSR and they had managed to attract in their orbit several other countries that used to have political and economic relationships with them. With the fall of communism in the Eastern European block and the consequent dissolution of the USSR, followed by the economic crisis of Russia of 1998, by the end of the twentieth century USA had eventually managed to become the only world superpower: its economic strength and military power had outclassed any other player both in the European and in the Asian block. The September 11 terrorist attack had even enhanced the US role as the custodian of world peace and undisputed military supremacy.

However, during the first few years of the new millennium the situation seems to be evolving towards the return of a bipolarization, where the US continues to be the leader, but a rising economic power in the Asian block seems bound to become a very important challenger: we are clearly referring to China, the fastest growing economy in Asia and possibly already the second largest economy when considered at P.P.P.[3]

With the creation of the European Union (EU) in the last decade of the past millennium, the old continent could have had the potential to become a very important geopolitical subject capable to contrast the dominance of America. However, both for internal political problems within the countries and within the Union (e.g., the failure of the European constitution) and for the slow down and loss of competitiveness of the major economies, the role of the EU on the international scenario has been rather limited during the last decade. In fact, an unbalanced implementation of the common currency creating hidden inflation in many European countries, the strengthening of the Euro vis-à-vis the dollar and the increased competitiveness of the imports form E.Cs have weakened the European economies and have created unemployment and discontent among their people. Consequently, a negative feeling towards the way the EU was developing has spread across the societies, causing internal problems in some countries, as well as detachment from the European institutions.

The fracture between the France–Germany axis and UK in the occasion of the 'war on terrorism' has further endangered the unity of the EU. Since some of the mentioned problems are structural, it looks therefore, unlikely that Europe will be able to take a lead role in the global geopolitics of the twenty-first century.

6.2.2 The Emerging Superpower

With the economic power, come also the political influence, the overall position among the most powerful nations and, more in general, in the global geopolitics.

For the USA, one of the main objectives of foreign policy, apart from the Iraq war and more in general the 'war on terrorism', seems to have recently become the containment of China: in the legislative branch of the US Congress since the year 2000, seven bodies, between agencies (two) and groups (five) were formed with a China related purpose. These are in addition to the long established Government Accountability Office and Library of Congress, Congressional Research Service, which 'have churned out a plethora of reports for Congress on US–China political and trade issues' (Seldin 2006).

While in the case of the USSR, the Cold War was mainly an ideological and military contention, in this case the main battleground is still, for the time being, economics. Yet it cannot be a true war, since, paradoxically, the USA as well as the whole world need China: the latter for its role as locomotive of the global economy; the former, as a large part of its international trade happens with China and because the 'Midway Empire' detains a considerable part of the US Public Bonds as well as a large amount of reserves in dollars (see Figure 6.1).

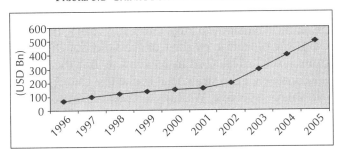

Today 80 per cent of the Wal-Mart suppliers are Chinese: this is even more surprising if we think that 10 years ago only 6 per cent of Wal-Mart products were not coming from the US (Fishman 2005).

An openly hostile approach to China may, therefore, give birth to a trade war or some monetary manoeuvers that might have the potential of dramatically hindering the American economy.

FIGURE 6.1 CHINA'S FOREIGN EXCHANGE RESERVES

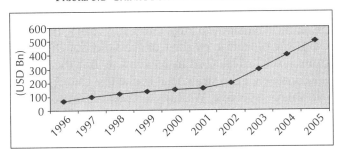

Source: Hang Seng Bank Limited, October 2005.

The rivalry with China is becoming increasingly higher, since clear symptoms of the impact on the US economy of the China growth are showing in several worrying ways. From the loss of jobs coming from factories being relocated (e.g., the town of Anderson in Indiana left over 20 thousand people jobless when a factory of General Motors was shut down[4]), to the heavy USA trade commercial deficit partly caused by the under-evaluation of the yuan, the last few years have completely changed the perception of China among the US Government foreign affairs policy makers. Following the advice provided by H. Kissinger during the seventies, President Nixon started the process of opening the doors to China. The relationship between the two countries became more intense with President Clinton, who had bet on the economic help to China in order to ensure its path towards democracy: the intention was actually correct, but the consequences of that decision are now boomeranging on America (see Table 6.2). After the takeover of the personal computer division of IBM by the Chinese Lenovo, an even clearer matter of concern has surfaced among the US Parliament members when the China National Offshore Oil Corporation has tried to buy Unocal, the energy company of the California state in July. After July 2005, the boycott of the operation by the Congress did not allow the Chinese firm to succeed in its venture, but the matter was considered the straw that broke the camel's back.

In this perspective, Washington seems now to have a clear strategy to implement the containment of China. The first pillar of this strategy is to gain the confidence and cooperation of the countries around China. The possible threat of a strategic partnership between China, Japan and India is among the worst possible scenario that may lead to the creation of a compact Asian block with immense economic and military potential. This would mean the loss of strategic position in Asia, the continent that is now seen as the rising star of the twenty-first century. Such scenario might become even more dangerous if the alliance had to include Russia also, emerging as a strong supplier of energy, one of the most precious elements for the growth of the economies. A close cooperation among these countries could have the potential to create a self-sufficient geopolitical area that could significantly obscure the leadership of the United States. Such a scenario is not so far from reality and the seeds of it have already been planted.

TABLE 6.2 CHINA'S TRADE WITH THE UNITED STATES (USD BILLION)

	1995	1996	1997	1998	1999	2000	2001	2002	2003	2004	2005
US Exports	11.8	12.0	12.8	14.3	13.1	16.3	19.2	22.1	28.4	34.7	41.8
% change	26.9	1.7	6.7	11.7	−8.4	24.4	17.8	15.1	28.5	22.2	20.5
US Imports	45.6	51.5	62.6	71.2	81.8	100.0	102.3	125.2	152.4	196.7	243.5
% change	17.5	12.9	21.6	13.7	14.9	22.2	2.3	22.4	21.7	29.1	23.8
Total	57.4	63.5	75.4	85.5	94.9	116.3	121.5	147.3	180.8	231.4	285.3
% change	19.3	10.6	18.7	13.4	11.0	22.6	4.5	21.2	22.7	28.0	23.3
US Balance	−33.8	−39.5	−49.8	−56.9	−68.7	−83.7	−83.1	−103.1	−124.0	−162.0	−201.7

Sources: US International Trade Commission, US Department of Commerce www.uschina.org

Note: US exports reported on FAS basis; imports on a general customs value, CIF basis.

One of these seeds is the SCO, or Shanghai Cooperation Organization, created in 2001 with the objective to ensure a closer cooperation between Russia, China and the Central Asian countries. According to the Chinese President Hu Jintao, the essence of the SCO is the 'Shanghai spirit', which embodies a new security concept calling for 'mutual trust and common security, partnership and non-alliance, openness and transparency, equality and consensus, mutual benefit, and not being against any third country or regional groups' (Bhadrakumar 2006). The two main countries of the cooperation have had period of good relationships as well as moments of extreme tension. It is said that at a certain time Moscow had planned a nuclear attack on China[5]. Recently there have been tensions about Chinese farmers settling down in the Asian part of Russia; but the issue seems now to have become an opportunity, since the Russian Far East is underpopulated (7 million inhabitants in 215 thousand square kilometres) while the bordering Chinese regions are highly overpopulated (100 million people in a much smaller area)[6]. Having forgotten the past problems, Russia and China have been regularly meeting within the SCO, sometimes inviting the neighbouring countries to join the talks. India was granted the status of observer within the SCO, and in the meeting that was held in Shanghai in June 2006, Iran has also been invited to become a permanent member. With Iran as part of the SCO, the alliance would control a major part of the world natural gas reserves, as well as a relevant part of the oil. Though the decision on this issue has been postponed, the invitation had sent a loud signal of willingness of the cooperation to become more and more self-sufficient from the energy point of view and with an independent line of thought, not necessarily aligned with the Western blocks.

In fact, while during the first three years of the alliance there was no major action resulting in visible changes in the area, since 2004, the scene has evolved. In July 2005, the leaders of Russia and China issued a joint declaration on 'world order' rejecting efforts by any power to achieve a 'monopoly in world affairs', divide the world into 'leaders and followers' and impose 'models of social development' on other countries (Weinstein 2005). The same declaration signed by all participants called for the closure of the US military bases in Uzbekistan and Kyrgyzstan: these were supposedly catering to the military operations in Afghanistan, but are in fact two important platforms of presence to oversee the East of Asia as well as East of Africa. The declaration has shown its effect, and the President of Uzbekistan has eventually decided to shut down the US military base in his territory.

It is therefore, clear why the USA has been since then fully engaged in seeking the cooperation of the countries neighbouring China, so as to create a 'safety belt' to counterbalance the increasing geopolitical weight of Beijing.

The second strategy used by Washington to protect its own interest vis-à-vis those of the rising rival concerns the surveillance of the seas and the territories of East Asia where the oil transit happens[7]. The USA is therefore trying to limit the influence of China on the islands of the East and South China Sea, as well as on the Malacca canal: their naval fleets have a constant presence in the region sailing between Malaysia and Singapore. The strategic importance of the oil supply was evident when the US strongly opposed the creation of the Iranian gas pipeline, which would supply gas from Iran to Pakistan and India.

The conversion of the countries surrounding China to the containment strategy is the third course of action being implemented by Washington. While Australia and Israel are the allied forces on which the Pentagon is confident to be able to count on, these countries stand at the border of the Asian continent: other countries with a closer proximity to China need to be taken along with the objective of ensuring a stronger position in Asia. Among these Japan, a historical rival of China; Taiwan, on the verge of a war with the Mainland; South Korea, strategically located; but above all India, which in the most recent years have become the ideal allies to counter-balance the Chinese power.

6.2.3 The Role of India

A number of reasons make India the best candidate to become the US strategic partner. First, the fast growth in the most recent years has increased the economic power of the nation; second, the increasing population of India, bound to overtake even the Chinese in a few decades ahead, constitutes a huge mid-term potential, both as a military force and as a talent pool; third, the fact of being a democracy with good internal stability and law and order situation is a non negligible factor in the US vision[8]. Not to forget also that India represents a stability factor also vis-à-vis the surrounding countries in South Asia, where Bangladesh, Nepal and Sri Lanka have shown continuous internal political problems; Pakistan is still a military regime (though on the road to become a democracy, according to its current leader) and so is Myanmar.

The change of the US approach towards India has been clear since July 2005, when the Indian Prime Minister visited Washington and was welcomed with the highest honors and invited to address the Congress. Later, the American Secretary of State visited India, and the tone of the talks held with the members of the government was extremely positive and open to maximum cooperation. In March 2006, President Bush visited India and sealed a nuclear deal, the foundations of which had already been laid in the mentioned meeting of July 2005. The US committed to provide to India the access to civil nuclear power technology versus the promise from India to separate military from civilian activities and open the facilities to inspections. While such a bill has already been approved by the US House of Representatives, it will also need the senate's approval to be ratified.[9] This marks the official acceptance of India among the World Nuclear Power Countries, a giant leap versus the sanctions following the Indian nuclear test of 1998.

Despite the recently consolidated partnership with the USA, India has stated several times in the past that, due to its multilateral vision of the world geopolitics, the country cannot accept the US unilateral foreign policy. For this reason, Delhi keeps improving its relationship with Beijing, in a strategy that could be defined as Double Engagement. In May 2006, the respective Ministries of Defense of the two countries signed an important Memorandum including joint military exercises and training programmes. On the other hand,

Washington, that had previously tried without success in 2003, started new attempts in June 2006 to involve Delhi in the international army contingent in Afghanistan. In April 2006, the Chinese and Indian Finance Ministers held talks in Delhi about removing roadblocks on trade and cooperating in the financial sector. During the same period another Chinese delegation had shared its views with the Indian Central Bureau of Investigation on anti-corruption measures. The bilateral trade between India and China keeps on growing: in the year 2005 the level of the same was more than six times that of the year 2000 (see Figure 6.2). The two countries seem to have understood that there are many sectors where they could become complementary rather than rivals (e.g., I.T., where the strength of Chinese hardware producers could use the well-developed expertise of Indian software designers). China is in fact considered the ideal base for manufacturing of goods; India the ideal one for outsourcing of services.

The visible attempt from the USA to establish a partnership with India is an additional reason for China to reinforce the links with India, and in order to avoid that, in case of conflicts with Washington, Delhi may take a defined stand to support the Western power. India is certainly interested in the support that America could provide, both in the nuclear issue and in sorting out the disputes with Pakistan (a former US ally) on Kashmir, and could get from the US also the decisive help to become a permanent member of the United Nations Security Council; however, a stronger cooperation with China could create strong synergies and help the country achieve even faster rates of growth, thus improving the nation's welfare. In fact, India shares

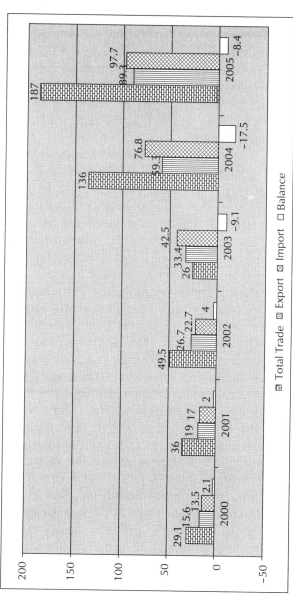

FIGURE 6.2 SINO-INDIAN TRADE BALANCE (USD100 MILLION)

Source: China's Customs Statistics/www.bjreview.com.cn

⊞ Total Trade ⊞ Export ⊠ Import ☐ Balance

Year	Total Trade	Export	Import	Balance
2000	29.1	15.6	13.5	2.1
2001	36	19	17	2
2002	49.5	26.7	22.7	4
2003	42.5	33.4	26	-9.1
2004	136	76.8	59.3	-17.5
2005	187	97.7	89.3	-8.4

with China also the urge to find the necessary scarce commodities (e.g., oil, steel) that are very important to sustain the growth experienced during the last few years.[10] In this direction they seem to be preparing a common offer to acquire some oil fields in Kazakhstan. China had already bought in 2005 the company PetroKazakhstan, which may be used in future to develop these fields.

India also enjoys good relation with Japan and the level of Japanese investments in India is already relevant. Both Japan as well as Taiwan look at India as an important ally in case of a possible conflict with China and this is another additional reason for the latter to increase the cooperation with the subcontinent.

The fact of being the centre of attention for the two rivals provides India the opportunity of selecting what best is offered. India becomes 'the swinging power' between USA and China: the one that will succeed to get Delhi on its side may have the highest chance to become the dominant world superpower of tomorrow. China had a similar role during the Cold War in the seventies, oscillating between the USSR and USA and it certainly paid back. In the meantime, the disputed country is playing its cards to acquire a higher visibility among the other major players in the international scene: its massive presence in January 2006 at the World Economic Forum in Davos proved the fact that the Indian government has eventually understood how to sell the attractive opportunities it has. Stability, democracy and talents were some of the key strengths displayed to attract possible investors: considering the increasing level of foreign investments flowing in the country, its strategy seems to be actually working.

6.2.4　Other Important Players

Apart from India, there are however, at least two more partners of considerable importance for China in order to secure a stronger position vis-à-vis the Western rival: Japan and Russia.

Japan had a controversial past in the first half of the twentieth century. Its victory in the war with Russia in 1905 marked the first success of an Asian country against a European one. However in the successive decades, its expansionist aims pushed the nation towards regional wars in China, Korea and South East Asia, which represented the preamble of the clash against the European nations and the USA.

After the humiliation of the Second World War the nation had worked hard to heal its wounds, re-building a devastated economy as well as its international image. The recovery was slow but constant and the efforts of the Japanese people resulted into a growing prosperity that led to the economic boom of the eighties. However by the end of the decade another economic crisis was to hit the country and last for over 15 years. Only by 2004, the first signs of a recovery started appearing and 2005 marked the first year of growth after a long period of deflation and slugging economy.

During the second half of the twentieth century, Japan became one of the major donors towards the E.Cs. The Constitution re-written by the Americans, post the defeat, prevented Japan to have an offensive army and forbade any military intervention in international conflicts: despite this, the nation played a major diplomatic role in some of them (e.g., in the conflict between the Sri Lankan Government and the LTTE rebels).

The relationship between Japan and China has always been rather complex: the economic ties are quite developed, the bilateral trade exceeds 170 billion USD and several thousand Japanese companies have their manufacturing units in China. However the political positions of the two countries are rather distant. This is comprehensible, given the history of conflicts between them and the aspirations of both to have a leadership role in the region. During the last decade, Japan has been often highlighting to the world the increasing military expenses of Beijing sustained by the booming economy, the lack of transparency of their military budget and the frequent violation of the sea and air territorial space by Chinese planes and ships.

In this picture it is easy to realize that the Pentagon sees in Tokyo, a crucial support in its strategy of containment. According to the rumours a secret go-ahead to build their own nuclear bomb would have already been agreed to between Washington and Tokyo. In November 2005, Japan changed its Constitution in order to be able to 'react to the possible conflicts which may occur in the coming fifty years'.[11]

One of the major grounds of tension between the two East Asian countries is the issue of historical memories. The visit regularly paid by the highest Japanese authorities to the Yasukuni Temple, where war criminals are worshipped cannot be accepted by China, that has experienced inhuman cruelties[12] by some of them. Another recent moment of tension happened in March 2005, when 30 million Chinese people signed a petition to the United Nations against Japan becoming a permanent member of the Security Council of the same. Other mass protests also occurred later in several

Chinese cities, damaging shops displaying Japanese products. This was the reaction to the proposal of the Secretary General to reform the multilateral organization by increasing the involvement of those who contribute most to the United Nations. Despite this, in June 2006, the news that Japan would restart the line of credit to China, interrupted a few months earlier because of the temple issue, seems a step towards the improvement of the relation between the two countries. A further improvement could have happened with the succession of Koizumi by Yukuda, whose ideas are in favour of a closer relationship with China; however his renunciation to the candidature and the appointment of Shinto Abe as incumbent has ruled out this perspective.

The other major player is Russia. Though the dissolution of USSR and the economic crisis at the end of the twentieth century have drastically reduced the geopolitical weight of the country, its military power remains among the strongest in the world. The strategic importance of Russia in the current scenario is also given by the abundance of natural reserves (oil and gas), which makes the nation a key supplier for the growing economies of the region, as well as for Europe (see Map 6.1).

The second half of the twentieth century had seen difficult relationships between China and Russia, culminating with the break-up of the same between Mao and Krusciov in 1964. A few years later, along the Sino-Russian border the banks of the Ussuri River saw harsh battles between the respective armies. The strong link between China and USA contributed in keeping the distance between Moscow and Beijing. More than 20 years later the Russian President Gorbachov visited

MAP 6.1 RUSSIA EUROPE GAS PIPELINES

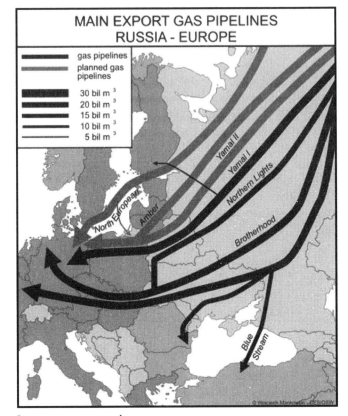

Source: www.osw.waw.pl

the Chinese capital in 1989. Ten years later, the dialogue between the two countries restarted when they discovered their common interest: containing American supremacy. The occasion was the Kosovo war, when an area previously under the Russian influence was attacked by the NATO; the supposedly 'accidental' bombing of the Chinese embassy in Belgrade made the anti-American feeling spark in China and pushed the countries to-gether against their common rival (Rampini 2006).

China bought weapons from Russia: it was through the Russian technical assistance that they could build their nuclear weapons. The countries carried out a massive joint military exercise in the summer of 2005 (see Map 6.2). They had created the SCO some years earlier (see Section 6.2.2), which has progressively gained political weight.

MAP 6.2 CHINA–RUSSIA JOINT MILITARY EXERCISES—AUGUST 2005

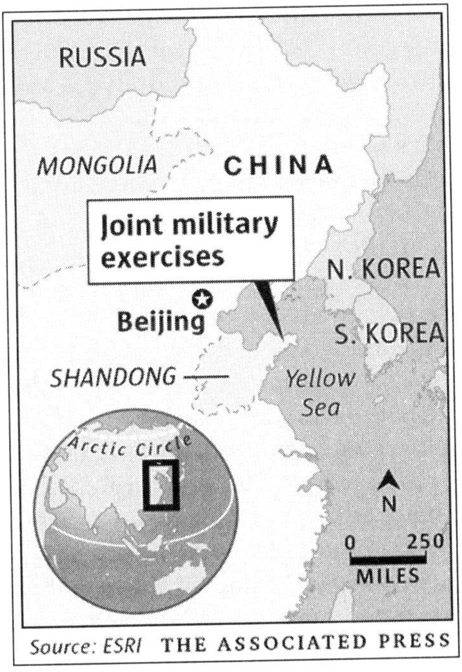

Source: ESRI THE ASSOCIATED PRESS

Source: www.freerepublic.com

After decades of turbulent relationship, the cooperation between China and Russia seems now to be at its best: this represents a threat for the USA, that started strengthening it's ties with the other countries of the region, both the historical friends (Australia and Thailand) and the previous enemies (Vietnam).

Apart from the improving relationship with China, Russia has also been active in the geopolitical scene with other potential partners. Algeria is one of them. Since a huge debt to Russia was cancelled by President Putin, the North African country has been buying weapons and defence system from the Eurasian partner. Also, Russia has been given access to the Algerian oil and gas fields, and the two national oil companies seem bound in a closer cooperation in providing energy to Europe. The relationship between Russia and Iran has already been highlighted while talking about the SCO earlier. Russia also supplies weapons of various degrees of sophistication to the Middle East country. Incidentally, despite this strengthening tie, it would seem that Gazprom, the Russian national gas monopolist, has entered into negotiations to supply gas through Turkey to Israel, among the fiercest enemy of Iran.

Within the Asian region, a relevant role is also played by the ASEAN countries, an alliance created in 1967 among the nations of South East Asia, originally comprising of five countries[13] which was later on extended to four additional ones. The association was borne as a cooperation of anti-communist countries, but later on included also communist countries such as Vietnam, with the objective of ensuring the regional stability and an integrated market.

China started to open a dialogue with the South East nations since 1995, by participating in some of the meetings of the same, sometimes together with Japan and South Korea. In November 2002, China signed an agreement to develop a free trade area with the ASEAN. But it was during the SARS crisis of 2003 that the ties between the two partners became much stronger. The Chinese Prime Minister participated in the emergency meeting of the ASEAN to discuss the SARS issue: the deliberations coming from the same and the intense joint activities of the subsequent months created a stronger relationship between China and the mentioned countries. Even in a situation that could have potentially caused a major setback, the emerging superpower managed to come out stronger and with reinforced links within the region.

6.2.5　The Two Contenders

The USA was a strong supporter of China during the Presidency of Clinton. One of the episodes that marked the turnaround of the political relationship between the two countries was the interception by the Chinese Air Force of a US spy aeroplane in the skies above the Hainan Island in the spring of 2001. The plane was made to land, held for sometime and after official apologies from the US Government, was released.

A few months later, post-September 11, Washington sought the cooperation of Beijing for the 'war on terror'. Within this war, China had a key role in handling the North Korean nuclear issue consequent to the inclusion by President Bush of the country in the 'axis of evil'.[14] Since May 2003, a renowned expert of China, Aaron Friedberg, has been co-opted in the American Ministry of Defence, as advisor for the National Security to the

Vice President. It was becoming more and more clear that the two countries would soon become strategic competitors.

The US strategy of containment towards China turned sharper in May 2006 in the attempt to keep under control the ever-increasing military expense of the Asian counterpart. At that moment, the American Department of Defense released a new dossier on the possible military threat from China, where the purchase of weapons from Russia, the modernization of their arsenal and the aspiration to have a major influence on the world geopolitics were loudly blamed. Some other direct or indirect statements were made by US vis-à-vis China. When in April 2006, President Hu Jintao visited Washington, he was not given the honour of a full state dinner, but only a short state lunch was organized for him.[15] Washington has also more than once accused Beijing of 'not playing by the rules' (Parsi 2006) while trying to control the energy sources: incidentally, it is rather surprising that such a statement may come from the country that has been trying to implement a similar strategy for the last few decades, to the extent of going to war in order to ensure its energy agenda.

Interestingly, Washington criticisms have covered also other countries other than China, for topics related to issues other than energy. In May 2006 during a speech in Lithuania the US Vice President declared that the Russian Government had '...unfairly and improperly restricted the rights of its people' (Ibid). In the same occasion he also blamed their energy policy. Similar comments on the lack of democracy was also made about the Arab Kingdom. All this does not facilitate the relationship between USA and these countries.

On the other hand, China keeps, in fact, extending her network of influence. The Gulf countries, historically linked with the US, seem to be on their way to rethinking this long-time alliance, mainly because of the Iran issue; China represents their alternative towards the creation of an autonomous safety regional block in good relationship with Iran. Proof of the closeness of the Chinese relationship with these countries has been the trip by President Hu Jintao to Riyadh in the spring 2006, when he was invited to address the highest authorities of the Kingdom. In parallel, the Saudi sovereign had previously visited Beijing in one of his first international missions.[16] The Gulf countries have had a long time relationship with South Asia: such a link has even strengthened, thanks to the issue of the Iran–Pakistan–India gas pipeline, which at a moment seemed likely to be extended to China also. The project was initially firmly opposed by the US, who later seemed to have changed their mind in an attempt to gain the support of India. The latter had clearly stated her willingness to proceed in the project despite the American veto. The closeness between India and Iran is one more reason why Washington has been trying hard to conquer Delhi's cooperation.

With the objective of securing new sources of energy, 'The Dragon' has also been active in the African continent, wherever possible oil suppliers could be found. Since the creation of the China–Africa Forum in 2000, China has scrapped tariffs on 190 imported goods from 28 African Countries and cancelled 1.2 billion USD in debt (Engdahl 2006). In Nigeria, the country with the largest ascertained oil reserves of the region, China has committed to restructure the obsolete railway network: in exchange drilling licenses will be granted. In Angola, another oil and gas producer, it has pledged two billion USD for infrastructure investment; in return, it has obtained a stake in oil exploration in the waters off their coast. In North Africa, it has signed an agreement for the construction of a highway.

On the other hand in another North Africa region, Libya, which had been for many years a strong US enemy, diplomatic relationships between the two countries have eventually been re-opened. This seems to have created concerns within the Chinese Government.

As we can see during the last decade both the rivals have been active in networking with the potential allied nations. However, the Iraq War (and to same extent the Iran issue), further to diverting the focus of the USA from other important areas, has prompted an increasing anti-American feeling in many countries and particularly among the Middle-East and other Islamic ones. At the same time, a period of high growth and increasing trade relationships with most of the developed countries are generating economic resources and political opportunities for the rising Eastern star.

Who will eventually gain the supremacy and how will depend on a number of factors, such as the outcome of the war in Iraq, the sorting out of the Iranian and North Korean issues, the sustainability of the Chinese growth, as well as the success in securing the support of the mentioned strategic countries. The end of the current decade will possibly provide the answer to these questions.

Notes

1. It is called The Global Brand scorecard. The methodology evaluates the brands on the basis of how much they are likely to earn in the future. The projected profits are discounted to get a present value and the risk profile of the earnings is assessed taking into account considerations such

as market stability and global reach. For details see http://
bwnt.businessweek.com/brand/2005/index.asp

2. They are Samsung and HSBC: the other 3 are EBay, Apple
   and UBS. See www.Finfacts.com/brands.htm
3. P.P.P. means Parity of Purchasing Power: it is a way of making
   different countries with different levels of prices and income
   comparable, by taking as reference the amount of goods that
   can be purchased in a certain country at a given time with
   a given amount of money.
4. See BBC World Business Report, 25 May 2005.
5. See Claudio Landi, *Buongiorno Asia*, 5 June 2006.
6. Ibid., 6 June 2006.
7. See 'Cindia, la sfida del secolo', 'Il segreto di Pasnak' , in
   Limes, Rivista Italiana di Geopolitica, September 2005.
8. See 'Cindia, la sfida del secolo', in *Limes*.
9. The discussion and vote in the Senate will take place in the
   last quarter of 2006.
10. The world steel production grew by 5.8 per cent during 2005:
    excluding China and India the output actually fell by 1.8 per
    cent (www.issb.co.uk).
11. Words from the speech of the Japanese premier to introduce
    the constitutional reform.
12. In the Nanjing massacre of 1937, the Japanese army is said
    to have killed hundred of thousands (300,000) Chinese
    people (the figures are debated by Tokyo); a unit of the
    Japanese army is said to have killed over 250,000 civilians
    in North China to experiment bacteriological weapons
    during the war of 1931.
13. Philippines, Indonesia, Thailand, Malaysia and Singapore.
14. The other countries mentioned by the American President
    in the so-called axis were Iraq and Iran.
15. See 'US outflanked in Eurasia Energy Politics', by F.W. Engdahl,
    on www.Atimes.com, 10 June 2006.
16. See Claudio Landi, *Buongiorno Asia*, 6 June 2006.

References

Aguaiar M., A. Bhattacharya, T. Bradtke, P. Cotte, S. Dertnig,
    M. Meyer, D. Michael, H. Sirkin. 2006. 'The New Global
    Challengers, How Top Companies from Rapidly Developing

Economies are changing the world', *BCG Report*, Boston Consulting Group, May.

Bhadrakumar, M.K. 2006. 'China and Russia Embrace the Shanghai Spirit', *Asia Times online*, 16 June.

Fishman, Ted C. 2005. 'China Inc.', on 'State of the World 2006', Worldwatch Institute.

Maitra, R. 2005. 'China's Shadow Over India's US Lobby', *Asia Times*, 13 September.

Parsi, T. 2006. Gulf Widens Between US and Sheikhdoms, http://www.Atimes.com

Pelle, S. 2004. 'Global and Local Brands', *Pearl of Wisdom*, vol. 2, Pune.

Rampini, Federico. 2006. *L'impero di Cindia*, Mondadori. SCMHRD.

Seldin, R. 2006. 'The US Finger on China's Pulse', *Asia Times online*, 16 June.

Weinstein, M.A. 2005. PINR, 'Intelligence Brief: Shanghai Cooperation Organization', 12 July.

Appendix 1

Financial Times
New Delhi, Friday, 17 March 2006

EU Curbs on Shoe Imports Attract only Three Votes

Only three of the 25 European Union member states yesterday voted in favour of a proposal to sanction cheap leather shoes made in China and Vietnam, highlighting a growing split in Europe about how to respond to booming Asian exports.

The outcome of the confidential vote in the EU's anti-dumping committee shows the difficulties facing Peter Mandelson, the EU's trade commissioner, as he tries to construct a trade policy that meets conflicting European demands and can withstand a possible challenge before the World Trade Organisation.

The proposal received the cold shoulder from an accidental coalition of countries seeking tougher curbs on imports to protect domestic producers, and others that oppose sanctions as unduly protectionist.

The three countries that voted in favour of the shoe curbs were the smaller member states Belgium, Slovakia and Malta. Nine countries voted against, including Sweden and the other Nordic countries, and Ireland and Slovenia, diplomats said.

Eleven countries abstained, led by Italy and other nations that are home to most of the traditional European shoemakers seeking EU sanctions against unfair competition from Asian rivals. Their refusal to support Mr Mandelson at this stage underlines unhappiness about his proposed exemptions made for sports and children's shoes, which they fear could give Asian producers a loophole to rebrand exports. Germany and Cyprus did not vote.

Thomas Östros, the Swedish trade minister, yesterday told the FT that Mr Mandelson should withdraw his proposal now, given the 'very unusual [voting] result'.

'The Commission should really reconsider its whole policy at this stage and how they work with anti-dumping measures. We need to strengthen the quality of anti-dumping investigations in order to regain the confidence of member states', he said.

Unice Criticises EU

Europe's main business federation, Unice, has attacked the European Commission for taking too defensive a position on agriculture in the Doha global trade talks, which it says is pulling down the level of ambition in liberalizing industrial goods, writes Frances Williams in Geneva.

Adrian van den Hoven, Unice's international relations director, said Unice had written a 'strong letter' to Peter Mandelson, European Union trade commissioner, criticising the EU stance at the World Trade Organisation ministerial meeting in Hong Kong in December.

'The agriculture negotiations hang over the heads of European business all the time', he said yesterday. 'Low ambition is simply not going to work for us.'

Mr Mandelson's office put a positive spin on the vote. It argued that it showed his plan represented the middle ground in a growing clash between more protectionist countries that demand tougher curbs, such as Italy and Spain, and liberal nations that have little or no shoe production and want European consumers to benefit fully from cheaper goods made in Asia.

The 'protectionist' camp also wanted Mr Mandelson to impose full sanctions at once so they would affect-pricing

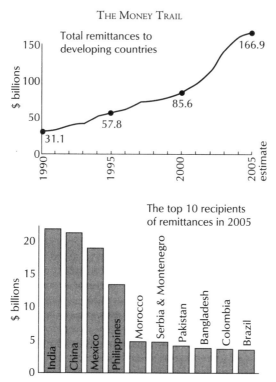

THE MONEY TRAIL

Total remittances to developing countries

166.9
85.6
57.8
31.1

The top 10 recipients of remittances in 2005

Source: World Bank.

before the next season's collection. Instead, he will introduce the sanctions in early April and gradually raise the duties to 19.4 per cent for China and 16.8 per cent for Vietnam.

Since the vote was only consultative, Mr Mandelson is proceeding with his plans and is expected to get formal backing from the EU executive on Wednesday. Mr Mandelson's office said he would then use the coming months to 'establish a consensus among member states on a definitive course of action', namely whether to prolong the sanctions by five years after October.

China has responded angrily to the proposed sanctions and warned that it could take the shoe issue before the WTO to expose 'serious flaws' in the data and arguments presented by Mr Mandelson to justify anti-dumping duties.

Raphael Minder in Brussels

Appendix 2

The Times of India
New Delhi, Tuesday, 29 August 2006

Gyanendra, Kin Hold Major Shares in 17 Firms: Probe

'He forced Govt. to pay millions to Royal Aunt for Murky Deals'

Kathmandu: Despite strenuous denials by at least two leading Indian joint ventures in Nepal—including tobacco giant ITC—a probe committee has informed the Nepal government that Gyanendra and his kin hold major shares in 17 companies.

Among the 17 companies whose yearly revenue is estimated to run into billions of rupees are Surya Nepal, ITC's venture in Nepal with British American Tobacco and a Nepali partner Hotel Soaltee Crowne Plaza, in which India's Oberoi Group has a 6% stake.

Also in the list is Himalayan Goodricke Private Ltd, a JV with India's Goodricke company and National Biscuit and Confectionery (P) Ltd, Nepal's first biscuit company in which India's Britannia Industries began technical collaboration from 1980.

The other 17 companies include a controversial five-star hotel, Hotel de l'Annapurna, in which the Taj Group of India held a stake but sought to divest it after pulling out of a management contract about two years ago, and a power company, in which the American investment company was forced to sell its shares to its Nepali partners after non payment of dues by the state-owned Nepal Electricity Authority.

Though Surya Nepal and Soaltee Crowne Plaza, which in the past were of 10 shut down by Maoists due to the royal link, always denied the connection, a parliamentary committee formed to detail the royal family's assets to bring them under the tax net, had the link corroborated on Sunday after the industry, commerce and supplies ministry sent in its report.

According to the preliminary report, though the majority shares in the companies were in the name of Gyanendra and his kin, a large percentage was transferred to his daughter Prerana and others during the 15-month direct rule of the monarch, apparently to hide the identity of the real owners.

A former royalist minister, his wife and the son of a former general and aide de camp were among such beneficiaries.

The culture of reciprocity and anonymity in business dealings flourished during Gyanendra's control, with the monarch compelling the government to pay millions to a royal aunt, Helen, ostensibly for medical treatment. But as the emerging facts show now, probably for her complicity in his murky business deals.

IANS

Appendix 3

The Bangladesh Observer
Dhaka, Monday, 3 April 2006

Why Industries Fail to Spread Roots

A top investor in the country's tourism sector is leaving the country out of frustration. So aghast is he with the administrative corruption, interference, harassment and bureaucratic tangle that he has at last decided to give up his effort to develop the country's tourism industry at international level. Before leaving for the USA, he gave vent to his feeling of utter disappointment with the bureaucratic system at a press conference. The entrepreneur with vast experience behind him has spoken not only of the awful condition he had to undergo but also made a case for others like him. His considerate opinion is that it is impossible for industries to flourish here under this condition.

As the owner of the only five-star hotel in Cox's Bazar and as a widely touring man, he possibly could do what he intended for tourism here. But what is significant is that he has painted a grim picture of the country's industrial sector. He pointed out the weakness in our industries and how that weakness becomes endemic. Entrepreneurs or industrialists cannot carry on their business freely even though they have to accept bank loans at high interests. At every step they have to satisfy different authorities and thus their industries become sick. Many of them turn loan defaulters and bankrupt. Indeed, there are more administrative manipulation than our naked eyes can meet.

Masum Iqbal, owner of the five-star Sea Gull at Cox's Bazar, has said so many things in his press conference: What he did not mention is the corrupt business cartel or syndicate that has developed over the years with blessings from the top political leadership. No wonder, the industrial base of the country has not shaped in any desirable manner; mostly the service sector without appreciable back-up linkage has spread its roots. All because a privileged section loyal to political coteries and having mutual stakes has tried to monopolise the economy of the country. These people have grown filthy rich and they have slammed the door in the face of any enterprising and honest person looking for an entry into business. Business has been too unclean here to draw really honest people.

Indeed, the corrupt influences of politics are now felt in every area of Bangladesh, but nonetheless it is not as strong in other areas as in the economic sector. After all, money has the power to make and unmake an individual, a society or even the country. Political corruption has taken a huge toll of the economy and economic corruption has taken in its turn an incalculable toll of Bangladesh society. The two are inseparable now.

The owner of the Sea Gull has done a good work by drawing the nation's attention to the problem facing the country in the industrial sector. Now it remains to be seen how the nation reacts to the matter. The fact that he wanted to put Cox's Bazar on the global tourism map in a more interesting way was not at all important to the people in power. They were interested to reap benefit from the initiative. Anyone with expertise and resources, he asserts, is highly appreciated in the USA but in Bangladesh all he received is cold shoulders from the government side. This is sad. Rhetoric that the government is ready to warmly welcome investors is one thing and the reality is completely different. Let the power wielders realise what a loss it would be to compel him to go. In the interest of the country, it is necessary to encourage investment in the private sector.

International Herald Tribune
Friday, 14 July 2006

Art of the Deal: It's Different in China

Cautious approach source of frustration

China Mobile Communications' planned purchase of Millicom International Cellular was such a sure thing that invitations had already been issued for a party in China to celebrate it.

Then, just hours before Millicom executives and advisers were to board planes to fly to Beijing to announce the $5.3 billion deal on July 3, the bad news started trickling in.

But it was not coming from China Mobile's bankers, or its top executives, with whom Millicom's team had been negotiating or months. Instead, the first sign that something was wrong came from news reports out of China, according to people close to Millicom, which is based in Luxembourg and has interests in cellular systems primarily in emerging markets. Millicom issued a statement later that afternoon that it had terminated 'all discussions concerning a potential sale', and its stock plunged more than 25 percent.

The demise of the closely watched deal, which would have been the largest overseas transaction for a Chinese state-owned company, is exposing a chasm between deal-making style in China and that of Europe and the United States. In China, many see China Mobile's last-minute exit as smart corporate strategy: Many analysts and deal makers say China Mobile narrowly avoided overpaying for a disparate group of assets.

In European and American deal-making circles, though, the way the exit was handled is prompting much frustration at investment banks and boardrooms. Had China Mobile warned Millicom earlier, it might have avoided upsetting the stock market, analysts say.

Some financial advisers warn that Chinese companies could find their buying prospects drying up. 'For a lot of prospective targets, they have lost credibility', said one European banker who spoke on the condition of anonymity because he did not want to alienate any prospective Chinese clients.

The debate comes at a time when Chinese companies' overseas strategy is being closely watched. Corporate China's outward expansion is pegged to a strategy of mergers and acquisitions, particularly of brand-name Western companies, but so far, transformational overseas deals have been scarce.

Wall Street's biggest investment banks paid multimillion-dollar salaries to hire Chinese bankers with top connections in recent years. While deal volume and equity offerings within the country have been brisk, big deals outside of China have been scarce, particularly outside of the energy sector.

Acquisitions by Chinese companies (not including Hong Kong-based companies) outside the country fell from $7.2 billion in 2004 to $4.9 billion in 2005, according to Thomson Financial. That is much smaller than the amount of external deals completed by companies in countries a tiny fraction of China's size. In 2005, Belgium-based companies bought $8.65 billion worth of companies outside the country, for example.

This year, Chinese companies are on track for record overseas deal-making, with over $9.8 billion in purchases completed already. Still, some bankers warn against the expecting a flood of big name overseas acquisitions. Chinese companies and managers are still getting used to deal-making, they say, and are by nature wary when it comes to large transactions. Some say the Millicom-China Mobile example may be the norm, rather than the exception.

Liang Meng, J.P. Morgan's co-head of China investment banking, expects just a few major deals out of China each year. The reason, he said, is largely because Chinese managers tended to proceed more slowly than many of their counterparts in the West before agreeing to go ahead with a transaction.

'They are more cautious, either because they have not done much of it or because they are entering into totally new markets or totally new environment', Meng said.

These executives have usually been in their job for 20 years or 30 years, much of that time solely inside China, and 'are becoming more international', he said.

'They have usually moved up because they are right most of the time or all of the time', Meng said, and they want to be absolutely certain a deal is the right move.

It should not be a surprise that despite Wall Street's heavy spending to hire bankers, merger volume has been subdued, according to some analysts.

'We are talking about a culture of doing business that has been learned over many centuries', said Jay Berry, a professor of business studies in China at Jilin University-Lambton College and a former McKinsey consultant.

Chinese companies are 'absolutely' slower than their foreign counterparts to do deals, Berry said. 'They are much absorbed by internal problems, tied to the wrong products, fragmented, unprofitable, uncompetitive, highly political and drowning in debt', he said.

The months of negotiations between China Mobile and Millicom were complicated and often frustrating for the European advisers and executives, who say their Chinese counterparts were difficult to pin down for meetings and that establishing a schedule to get the deal done was impossible. 'If they agreed to a date, they seemed to see that as a concession', one adviser said.

Veteran China deal makers found their European colleagues discomfort amusing and say they encountered a common negotiating tactic.

'When Kissinger and Nixon went to China, they didn't know when they were going to meet Mao', said jack Huang, head of the greater China practice at the law firm Jones Day. 'That game has been played by the Chinese over and over.'

Still, Huang cautioned against saying that Chinese executives would not be able to close deals overseas.

'The Chinese know very well if you want to do deals on the international arena, you have to move expeditiously', he said. 'This is not a situation where the bureaucrats don't know the realities outside of China.'

Still, Chinese companies are operating at a disadvantage to their multinational competitors on the deal-front. Multi-national companies outside China generally have a special team that deals with mergers and acquisitions, said Oded Shenkar, author of 'The Chinese Century' and a professor of management at Ohio State University.

'They have experience and routines as to how you look at a deal, and they'd abort it fairly early on' if it was not going to work, he said. 'The Chinese do not have that yet', Shenkar said.

In the past year, China's successful big-ticket deals were in the energy sector, including the $4.5 billion purchase PetroKazakhstan by China National Petroleum, the parent of PetroChina, and the $1.42 billion purchase of Ecuadorean oil fields by Andes Petroleum.

Top executives in the sector are used to deal-making, some advisers. Andes management is a 'sophisticated team', said Angus Barker, UBS's head of mergers and acquisitions for Asia. UBS advised Andes on the Ecuadorean deal. Judging from the energy transactions, Chinese companies have 'shown they can mix it with all comers from around the world in auctions and win', Barker said.

Heather Timmons and Donald Greenlees

The Moscow Times
Thursday, 16 March 2006

Russia As a Prime Investment Destination

Business experts' opinion: Which challenges do companies face in Russia?

Russian businessmen often blame high political risks, which 'scare away' their foreign partners, but companies themselves don't focus attention on proper corporate governance, 'transparent' shareholder structure and putting accounting into

the requirements of IAS. Taking into account global investment funds standards being common for all the countries, a
company needs to demonstrate its striving to 'speak a common language' with the funds—the language of figures and
ratings supported by 'Big 4' audit companies and key international rating agencies.

Pavel Neumyvakin, CEO, 'Uniastrum Bank'

Russia amazingly combines features of an emerging market
having a low awareness of IP matters and a high piracy rate,
with characteristics of a developed market having a developing middle class and high purchasing power for consumer
electronics, PCs, and, of course, software. As a result, any software company working on the Russian market sooner or later
faces a number of challenges linked to IPR and its protection.

Piracy takes a number of forms in Russia—and software
producers can suffer from some, if not all, of them. Examples
include direct counterfeiting (CD production and distribution through street resellers, flea markets and on-line shops),
corporate mislicensing (one license bought, but products
installed and used at a number of PCs), casual copying (software exchange among friends), hard disk loading (illegal copy
pre-installation on new PCs), internet piracy (unlimited host-
ing at internet sites free of charge or for little fee without
permission from the IPR owner).

Despite all of the above, the situation is clearly changing.
IPR legislation has evolved significantly over the last several
years and today protects the interests of IP owners. The government is also paying recognizable attention to the piracy
problem: A governmental IPR commission was formed recently, and there is a police department focused specifically
on computer and software crimes. During the last two years,
the share of unlicensed PCs (with no legal software pre-
installed) shipped to Russia decreased more than 20 percent.
Today, more than half of all PCs coming to Russia have legal
operating systems pre-installed. We expect in the coming
years that the share of unlicensed PCs will keep falling.

According to the research agency Information Data Corporation, piracy has continuously decreased the last 10 years and there is potential for its further decrease. Although some significant challenges exist and IPR owners must address them with the appropriate resources, the opportunities for software market players today and in the near future are significant and worth the effort.

Sergey Alpatov, LC Manager, Microsoft Rus

We feel that the market in Moscow is fairly well developed and that St. Petersburg is a place where opportunities have been missed in the past. By bringing together a fund of such size—which is going to be about $50-100 million—this gives us the opportunity to invest in larger projects and to work with the city government on a scale that hasn't been done in St. Petersburg in the past, especially by a Western firm.

We've really seen a lot of positive reforms which have helped us to do business on the scale that we now hope to do. The (project in Sestroretsk) is a way to modernize existing brownfield sites which have been underutilized in the city, where you have industrial properties sitting on prime real estate. The changes in legislation have allowed us to work with the city government and some of the factories to purchase this land and redevelopment it in a way that is beneficial obviously to us and to the city.

What are some of the misconceptions that people not doing business in Russia have? There is a desire of the city government to develop St. Petersburg. The city is actively working, and generally transparently working, to try and make this process work smoothly and to work with foreign investors. They are actively courting foreign investors and eager to make this experience as smooth and worthwhile as possible.

Mac Broderick, Jensen Group

The Overseas Private Investment Corporation (OPIC) has been helping U.S. businesses invest in Russia since 1992—approving more than 140 finance and political risk insurance projects, worth more than $4.5 billion, in the last 13 years. Currently we have approximately $475 million invested in

Russia, and each year since 2001 we have seen an increase in the number of approved projects. For instance, in 2004 we approved seven projects for Russia and in 2005 we approved 14 projects.

Given that our core mission is to foster economic development in emerging markets, the most interesting development regarding Russia as a destination for U.S. direct investment is that we see increasing interest in relatively underserved regions. Last year we supported projects in Novosibirsk, Samara, Yekaterinburg and Vladivostok, and we anticipate that this trend will continue. We were also interested to see that all of our projects last year were outside of natural resource sectors and were primarily sponsored by small- and medium-sized American enterprises and investors.

Because OPIC works to support U.S. investment—I think it is fair to say that our growing and diversifying portfolio of projects here is an indicator that Russia is increasingly popular as a destination for American direct investment. This is also true when we compare Russia to other countries. In 2005, OPIC approved more projects in Russia than in any other country in which it works.

The Advertising Supplement did not involve the reporting or editorial departments of The Moscow Times.

Michele R. Smith, Investment Services Manager, Russia & CIS, Overseas Private Investment Corporation (OPIC)

Appendix 4

The Times of India
Mumbai Edition, Sunday, 9 April 2006

Chinese Piggyback on Hamara Bajaj Again

New Delhi: Imitation, they say, is the best form of flattery. But for India's largest two- and three-wheeler maker Bajaj Auto, it's more of a wake-up call—to stand up and protect a brand that's been a household name in India for decades.

Last week, the brass at Pune-based Bajaj Auto was jolted by a new threat—a lesser known Chinese rival which was making and marketing CNG three-wheelers in dragon land under the brand name 'Bajaj'.

This is not the first time that Bajaj Auto has faced a copycat problem from China. A few months back, the firm had come across another Chinese manufacturer, which had built a carbon copy of its top-seller bike, Pulsar, and was marketing it in Latin America under the brand name Gulsar.

'It was a rude shock for us. The company was actually making CNG three-wheelers and marketing them as China-made Bajaj autorickshaws', says a company source.

The Chinese copy—built by Gaongqing Union Auto Co— has nearly the same dimensions as the Indian original. But the Chinese have gone a step forward and are offering the product in custom-built options as well.

Although Bajaj Auto MD Rajeev Bajaj says efforts are on to track the copycat and raise intellectual property rights issues with the firm, industry insiders say it's easier said than done. 'It's a country that thrives on copycats. Even global brands like GM and Yamaha have not been able to stop sales of copies of their vehicles. It won't be easy for Bajaj either', says an analyst.

Byas Anand/TNN

The Moscow Times
Tuesday, 21 March 2006

Chinese to Make Their Own Volvos

Volvo hopes the move will help to make up for its late entry into the market

BEIJING—Ford's Volvo said Monday that it would begin making cars in China this year, a step into the world's third-largest car market that other up-market automakers took years ago.

Chief executive Fredrik Arp said Volvo would build its S40 sedan at a plant owned by Changan Ford, a Ford joint venture in the southwestern city of Chongqing.

While Volvo conceded it was late in entering a increasingly difficult market where profit margins were shrinking, the company was confident Chinese manufacturing operations would be profitable as early as next year.

Volvo said it could reach its Chinese manufacturing target of 10,000 cars per year in 2007, and was working with a number of Changan Ford's local suppliers to meet the government's local content requirements and the company's quality standards.

'We are, after working with [Changan Ford] on this project for over a year, convinced that their factory, working together with our own experts, can produce the quality Volvo requires', Arp told reporters.

'At 10,000 units, we will be making money', said Alexander Klose, head of Volvo's Asia Pacific operations.

Changan Ford is a joint venture between the second-largest U.S. carmaker and Changan Automobile.

Even with the recent strong growth in China sales, Volvo still lags behind its global rivals, such as Volkswagen's Audi, which has been making expensive cars for years for an increasingly cash-rich and style-conscious Chinese middle class.

Volvo's unit sales in China almost doubled in 2005 to over 4,800 units, and could more than double this year to 10,000. The company also sees significant growth for the foreseeable future.

'There is as good possibility it could double again next year', Klose said.

BMW set up its China factory in 2003, and Daimler Chrysler is building a plant in Beijing that will be able to build 25,000 Mercedes-Benz cars annually.

Chinese car sales grew 15 percent in 2004, after almost doubling in 2003, and analysts expect growth of 10 percent to 15 percent this year.

Even as overall growth slows, global manufacturers are confident China's dynamic economy will continue to produce more customers for higher-end cars.

'China will probably be the most important car market within five to 10 years in the world', Arp said. 'To be an importer only is not a long-term strategy.'

Rising competition is also eating into profits, turning a once lucrative market into one where high volume replaces high profits.

'The profit margins in this market are not outstanding in any direction', Klose said. 'China is becoming a regular market.'

After reviewing the China manufacturing operations at the end of next year, Volvo will reassess the market and determine if expanding output—which could include other models besides the S40—is justified.

'We will manufacture this car. We'll see how it works. We'll see how we are doing next year', Klose said.

Kirby Chien, Reuters

The Times of India
New Delhi, Wednesday, 26 July 2006

Tata, Fiat to Form JV for Cars

New firm to roll out grande punto; also plans to explore venture in Argentina

Mumbai/New Delhi: The Tata-Fiat alliance is moving into second gear. The automobile majors have agreed to form a JV to manufacture passenger cars, diesel engines and transmissions for the Indian and overseas markets. The firms have also agreed to explore possibilities of a similar partnership in Argentina.

The JV—to be based in Ranjangaon (Pune)—is expected to begin production of a premium compact car, the Fiat Grande Punto by early 2008. This will be followed by a new Fiat sedan. Tata Motors, which is running out of capacity at its own plant in Pune, will also manufacture its cars at the facility.

Though the firms did not divulge investment required for this project, experts believe it could be upwards of Rs 2,500 crore. Ravi Kant, managing director, Tata Motors, said, 'The details of the joint venture like the investments are being worked out and we will be in a position to talk of it when the agreement is formalised. The companies will hold equal stake in JV.'

The Ranjangaon facility, when it operates at full capacity, will roll out 1 lakh cars and 2.5 lakh engines and transmissions per annum. De Filippis Giovanni managing director Fiat India said, 'Diesel engines from the Ranjangaon plant will also be supplied to Tata cars manufactured at their Pune plant.'

Fiat is considering to 'optimise' its plant at Kurla, in Mumbai. De Filippis said, 'We have faced a lot of problems with the Kurla plant and there is a lot of idle capacity here. The plant and the operations are currently being reviewed.'

The two car makers announced that they will undertake a 60-day study on the possibility of industrial and commercial co-operation in Latin America, which traditionally has been a big market for the Italian automaker.

Times News Network

Appendix 5

Financial Express
Sunday, 22 January 2006

A Joy Ride for Kids

Gulf oil undertakes a rally to brighten up the lives of children

In an attempt to bring cheer to the lives of orphaned children, Gulf Oil Corporation Ltd is flagging of its CSR initiatives this year with Gulf Foster a Child Rally today. This is an annual event by the company.

This year two orphanages in Mumbai, Our Lady's Home for boys and St Anthony's Home for the girls, have been chosen. The initiative involves taking a child from the orphanage in a car by a family that would like to spend a day with the child. Essentially, this is for rallyists or other sports enthusiasts.

The route of the drive is simple: All one needs is a car. In each vehicle a family will drive with an orphaned child. In return, the company will give a donation to the orphanage in kind. Sportscraft, the organisers of the event, have decided to donate the amount received by way of entry fee to the orphanages.

Says N C Sekharan, head of Lubes, Gulf Oil Corporation Ltd, 'We will utilise this drive as a platform to spread awareness against orphaned and homeless children. This drive will not only provide an opportunity to the destitute kids to enjoy, but also be an occasion to instill compassion in the child of the participating family.'

Today, 50 children will be off in 50 cars, while other 50 children will ride in a bus, sponsored by Gulf Oil. At the end of the journey in Lonavla, the children will be treated to luncheon, magic show and gifts, et al. The company has planned this as a one-day event. Is it fair to the child who has to go back to his Gulf Oil employees with the children mundane daily activity the next day? 'We have plans to sponsor these children on a long-term basis', he says.

The company's employees are also involved in this annual event. 'Some of our employees sponsor the child's education, but we don't really get into the details' he says.

Sulekha Nair

Financial Times
Thursday, 11 May 2006

Fresh Corruption Charges Target Brazil's Deputies

The year-old corruption scandal surrounding the government of Luiz Inácio Lula da Silva, Brazil's president, has taken a fresh turn with accusations that a third of the lower house of Congress received bribes to make amendments to the country's national budget.

The accusations were made by Maria da Penha Limo, a former health ministry employee, who was arrested last week, along with 54 other people in a federal police operation known as Operation Bloodsuker.

Investigators had uncovered a scheme in which 170 federal deputies allegedly used budget amendments to release money to buy ambulances for local health authorities. The ambulances were bought for between a quarter and a third of the amount released and the remainder of the funds were allegedly shared among the scheme's operators.

Veja, a news magazine, ran a story containing transcripts of police recordings of telephone conversations between alleged operators of the scheme. They identify aides of members of Congress discussing the payment of bribes. In one conversation an aide discusses with one of the operators the possibility of killing a journalist investigating the affair.

Ms da Penha's accusations, made as part of a plea bargain, takes the case further. Her lawyer said she told investigators that members of Congress received 10 to 15 per cent of the amount they released through budget amendments, in a scheme understood to have involved at least R$110m ($53.5m, £41.9m, £28.7m).

Opposition leaders seized on the allegations as further evidence of widespread corruption in government. Members of Mr Lula da Silva's administration have been accused over the past year of using illegal campaign finance and of paying bribes to their congressional allies in exchange for their support in Congress.

'This is the theme of the Lula government', said Geraldo Alckmin, likely to run as candidate for the opposition centrist PSDB in the presidential election due in October.

Separately, the former secretary of Mr Lula da Silva's Workers' party gave evidence to a Senate corruption inquiry yesterday following a newspaper interview in which he put Mr Lula da Silva among decision makers in the PT when the cash-for-votes scheme was allegedly at its height. Mr Pereira refused to elaborate on his interview in the first part of his evidence, saying that he had not yet read the newspaper interview and so could not comment on it.

Jonathan Wheatley in São Paulo

The Moscow Times
Monday, 15 May 2006

Heads Roll in Anti-Corruption Drive

Ten senior law enforcement officials were fired Friday as part of President Vladimir Putin's anti-corruption pledge.

Major Generals Yevgeny Kolesnikov and Alexander Plotnikov, both Federal Security Service deputy heads, were let go Friday, Interfax said. A third Federal Security Service officer, Lieutenant General Sergei Fomenko, was also fired.

Kolesnikov and Plotnikov dealt with counterterrorism and anti-constitutional activities. Fomenko was the head of the department responsible for fighting drug trafficking.

Other terminations included those of Mikhail Nikonov, first deputy prosecutor at the Moscow Prosecutor's Office, and six senior Interior Ministry officials. One of those was Sergei Minasyan, the transport police chief of Adler airport.

The airport, which serves Sochi, was the destination of an Armenian plane that crashed earlier this month in the Black Sea, killing all 113 on board.

Separately, Alexander Zherikhov, head of the Federal Customs Service, was fired Friday, one day after Putin moved the service from the Economic Development and Trade Ministry and put it under the direct control of Prime Minister Mikhail Fradkov. Andrei Belyaninov, one of Putin's KGB colleagues from his days in East Germany and the current head of the Federal Service for Defense Contracts, replaces Zherikhov.

More people are likely to be fired, Putin suggested. 'The work in not over, and not only within customs', Putin said in televised remarks.

Putin said the dismissals were not meant to coincide with his state-of-the-nation address, in which he touched on corruption. 'When I was working on the address, I knew that work [related to the dismissals] was under way', Putin said.

The president suggested the Federal Security Service, or FSB, played a central role in all of the terminations.

Spokespersons for the affected agencies who could be reached by telephone declined to comment.

Pro-Kremlin political analyst Gleb Pavlovsky said the shake-up showed Putin was serious about tackling corruption.

Georgy Satarov, head of Indem, a think tank that deals with corruption-related issues, was skeptical of what the shake-up would bring. 'It's battling corrupt individuals, not corruption', Satarov told Interfax. 'The system needs to be changed'.

Andrei Soldatov, an independent security analyst, said the terminations reflected, above all, the FSB's mounting influence and internal changes at the security agency.

A counterterrorism law signed by Putin in March made the National Anti-Terrorist Committee the top panel for coordinating anti-terrorism activities. The panel is headed by FSB chief Nikolai Patrushev.

The new law also put regional FSB chiefs in charge of anti-terrorism efforts, meaning that in the event of a terrorist incident, all security operations would be run by FSB officials.

The FSB's growing influence was also reflected in the choice of Belyaninov as head of the Federal Customs Service, given that Belyaninov worked with Putin in the KGB's Dresden office in the 1980s.

Ruslan Pukhov, director of the Moscow-based Center for the Analysis of Strategies and Technologies, called Belyaninov a 'cashier' who paid Putin his monthly salary.

Belyaninov's tenure at Rosoboronexport, the state arms-trading monopoly, from November 2000 to April 2004, 'undoubtedly' played a role in his appointment, Pukhov said. His record at the Federal Service for Defense Contracts, which he has headed since leaving Rosoboronexport, also helped him, Pukhov said.

'His task there was to act as a watchdog over how the military brass spent money', Pukhov said of Belyaninov's work at the Federal Service for Defense Contracts. 'He was partially successful with this, but not as successful as his work with Rosoboronexport.'

The appointment solidifies the control of the clan of current and former security officials, many of whom come from St. Petersburg, known as the siloviki, said political analyst Vladimir Pribylovsky, head of the Panorama think tank.

Pribylovsky said the appointment would do nothing to curb corruption. 'The corruption will remain, but the money will be going to a different clan'. Pribylovsky. said.

In a related move, Sergei Mironov, speaker of the Federation Council, has taken steps to remove from power Boris Gutin, the representative of the Yamal-Nenets autonomous district legislature; Igor Ivanov, of Primorye region; Arkady Sarkisyan, of the republic of Khakasia; and Alexander Sabadash of the Nenets autonomous district.

Stanislav Belkovsky, director of the Council for National Strategy think tank, said Gutin and Ivanov were involved in customs-related 'schemes'. Sarkisyan and Sabadash, he said, are being punished for carving out their own power bases within the security agencies.

Carl Schreck and Valeria Korchagina
Staff Writers

Appendix 6

South China Morning Post
National, Tuesday, 18 July 2006

Hu Hails 'Practical' Three-way Talks

Common issues with leaders of India and Russia make for easy consensus

China, India and Russia hailed an unprecedented three-way meeting on common issues of energy, economic development and fighting terrorism yesterday as a step towards stronger ties.

The meeting between President Hu Jintao, Russian President Vladimir Putin and Indian Prime Minister Manmohan Singh came amid a series of bilateral and multilateral talks Mr Hu held on his last day in the Russian city of St Petersburg with leaders of G8 countries and counterparts from invited developing countries.

Speaking after the meeting at Constantine Palace, Mr Hu said: 'The three countries had a very practical discussion. The most important thing is we have so many common interests which help us reach consensus easily.'

By consensus, the Chinese president was referring to global energy security, education for innovative societies in the 21st century and the fights against infectious diseases and terrorism.

'After today's meeting, I believe that we can further develop our ties with each other very well', Mr Hu said.

Mr Putin reiterated the importance of China's and India's participation at the Group of Eight summit. 'Without China's and India's participation, the G8 summit couldn't have a successful and comprehensive discussion on economic and security sectors', he said.

Jiang Yuechun, director of the Division of World Economy at the China Institute of International Study—a Foreign Ministry think-tank—said the close ties between China, Russia and India meant more clout for developing countries when they co-operated with rich countries on the international stage.

'We know the three countries have a similar standpoint on fighting terrorism and other common-interest issues', Professor Jiang said.

Although Mr Hu and Mr Putin had met at least five times in the past year, both leaders also took time to meet separately before Mr Hu heads back to Beijing.

Professor Jiang said this was because China and Russia were traditional strategic partners and had many mutual interests.

'Sino-Russian relations have been built on traditional friendship and common interests, especially on how China's soaring economic development has needed Russia's energy support', he said.

'It is very common for the two leaders to be so close when they appear at various occasions on the international stage.'

Gui Yongtao, an expert from Peking University's Faculty of International Relations, said it was very important for the three countries to make commitments on energy security and the fight against terrorism.

He said the fight against terrorism could not succeed without the co-operation of the three countries because they were also three rising powers, and India was set to follow in China's footsteps as a rapidly developing economic force.

'China and India will co-operate with G8 but also keep their distance from it', Mr Gui said.

He added that the time was not yet for China to join the 'rich men's club.'

Minnie Chan in St Petersburg

The Times of India
New Delhi, Friday, 16 June 2006

Nicholas Piramal to Buy Pfizer's UK Unit

To become the largest contract manufacturer for American pharma major

Mumbai/New Delhi: Pharmaceutical major Nicholas Piramal India Ltd (NPIL) has struck a deal to acquire one of Pfizer's plants in Britain for an undisclosed amount. The transaction, which makes NPIL the largest contract manufacturer for Pfizer, is expected to be completed by the weekend. It is also expected to boost revenues by $350 million over the next five years.

The deal includes a supply agreement with Pfizer, which will continue to buy drugs from the plant, at Morpeth in northeastern England, until 2011. Nicholas Piramal's UK unit, NPIL Pharmaceuticals (UK), will acquire the Morpeth facility on an asset purchase basis. The acquisition will be funded through internal accruals.

The announcement lifted Nicholas Piramal shares to an intra-day high of Rs 172.5 on the BSE on Friday. The scrip closed nearly 8% higher at Rs 168.1.

The Morpeth site is one of Pfizer's integrated facilities, and houses end-to-end production and supply chain capabilities that cover active pharmaceutical ingredients, finished dosage, packaging and distribution. Pfizer's website states that, the plant, set up in 1960s, manufactures drugs for pain control, arthritis and ulcer prevention.

'As the facility has USFDA and UK MHRA nods along with a packaging division, it will help us sell products in 106 countries', said Ajay Piramal, chairman, NPIL. The deal will make Nicholas Piramal the biggest supplier within Pfizer's global contract manufacturing network. It will also help Nicholas emerge as one of the world's top 10 pharma outsourcing companies with manufacturing revenue exceeding $200 million a year.

'We expect revenues to be around half a billion for current fiscal, after the deal. Also, contract manufacturing segment will contribute 50% to revenues', Piramal said.

Times News Network

The Times of India
New Delhi, Tuesday, 6 June 2006

'There's Need for Better Ties With India'

Playing down the strained ties with China and South, Shinzo Abe, the chief cabinet secretary, has emphasised the importance of strengthening diplomatic ties with Asian countries, like India and Australia, that have 'common values' with Japan.

In a recent interview with the *Nihon Keizai Shimbun,* Japan's major economic daily, Abe said that Japan would continue to do business with China, but called China a destabilizing factor in Asia.

'We don't share basic values like freedom and human rights', he said. 'If you ask me whether the rule of law is established there, it's not.'

By contract, in a recent speech, Yasuo Fukuda, a former chief cabinet secretary, said that Japan needs to revise its policy toward the rest of Asia.

Mentioning the Asia policy that was carried out by his father, Takeo Fukuda, a prime minister in the 1970's, he said that Japan must resume 'heart-to-heart' dialogue with its neighbours and ultimately build an East Asian community.

Norimitsu Onishi
NYT News Service

The Times of India
New Delhi, Wednesday, 14 June 2006

China Moving Up the Trust Ladder?

Neither are we a threat to them, nor are they a threat to US, says Pranab

New Delhi: In the not too distant past, one defence minister (read George Fernandes) famously dubbed China the 'potential threat number one' for India. His successor, Pranab Mukherjee, however, is now all gung-ho over embracing the Red Dragon as a strategic partner.

Though the normally hawkish Indian defence establishment still keeps a watchful and concerned eye on the ever-growing Chinese military activity in the Tibetan Autonomous Region as well as the Indian Ocean, there is now a palpable sense of easing of tensions.

The 'threat perception' from China is now considered to be the lowest ever since the 962 conflict, with the possibility of an armed conflict not figuring on the radar screen at all. 'Neither are we a threat to them (China), nor are they a threat to us', says Mukherjee.

'We do believe there is enough strategic space for both of us to develop', said Mukherjee, who has just returned from a trip to China, which saw him travelling to military establishments at Beijing, Dunhuang, Lanzhou and Shanghai.

Moves are now afoot in South Block to institutionalise defence and military exchanges, including training programmes and joint exercises with the 2.5 million-strong People's Liberation Army (PLA), which is more than double the size of the Indian forces.

Towards this end, Chinese military observers have already witnessed an Indian armoured exercise in Rajasthan. There are now plans to hold joint exercises with PLA, possibly in the counter-terrorism arena, say sources.

As per the MoU signed between Mukherjee and his Chinese counterpart Cao Gangchuan on May 29, the two countries will now have an annual defence dialogue for 'a frank exchange of views on all military matters of mutual concern.'

Ask Mukherjee about the well-known Chinese help to Pakistan in its nuclear and missile programmes and he brushes it aside. 'We are aware Pakistan received some support from China in its various programmes, including weapons. At the same time, it has to be recognised that they (China) are interested in developing defence cooperation with India', he said.

What about the rapidly-modernising PLA, with its armoury of nuclear-tipped missiles? 'They have their own programmes, we have ours...But nobody is thinking in terms of an armed conflict. The basic understanding is that it's better to live in peace than in tension', said Mukherjee.

The CBMs along the unresolved 4,057 km Line of Actual Control (LAC) with China, despite occasional pinpricks by PLA, are on a firm footing. 'They will be further strengthened', said Mukherjee.

The military protocol signed during Chinese Premier Wen Jiabao's visit here in April 2005, in fact, goes far ahead of the earlier November 1996 agreement on maintaining peace and tranquility along the LAC. It lays down that the two armies will 'exercise self-restraint' and take 'all necessary steps' to avoid any escalation on the LAC.

The steps include immediate cessation of activities, no threat or use of force, return to bases and informing their respective HQs. The protocol also tackles air intrusions in a similar fashion, with flag meetings within 48 hours for seeking clarifications.

Rajat Pandit/TNN

The Times of India
New Delhi, Friday, 16 June 2006

Enter, The Dragon

Ahmadinejad in China for N-programme support

Shanghai: Iranian president Mahmoud Ahmadinejad arrived in Shanghai, renewing the focus on the role China may play in resolving the standoff over the Islamic republic's nuclear programme.

In a suggestion that China was concerned the Iran issue would overshadow everything else at the Shanghai Cooperation Organisation meeting, officials seemed eager not to play up expectations. 'I don't believe having discussion or not having discussion of the Iran nuclear issue is the determinant of the relevance of this conference', foreign ministry spokesman Liu Jianchao told a briefing in Shanghai.

Ahmadinejad is only a guest at the summit of the Shanghai Cooperation Organisation, which groups China, Russia, and four Central Asian states. Iran is an observer nation along with Pakistan, India and Mongolia.

Russian president Vladimir Putin, Pakistan's Pervez Musharraf and the leaders of Kazakhstan, Kyrgyzstan and Tajikistan and Uzbekistan were all in town for the meeting. But attention was expected to be on Ahmadinejad more than anyone else with the hardline Iranian leader slated to hold his first meeting with Chinese president Hu Jintao on Friday following the summit.

It was unclear what might be achieved by the talks in regards to Iran's nuclear programme, argued David Zweig, a China expert at Hong Kong's University of Science and Technology. It's good to have the two leaders sit and make Ahmadinejad understand the need not to go down the nuclear road, he said.

AFP

Moscow, Tehran to discuss nuke mess

St Petersburg: Russian president Vladimir Putin will meet with Iranian president Mahmoud Ahmadinejad on the sidelines of the summit of the Shanghai Cooperation Organization in that Chinese city, presidential aide Sergei Prikhodko said.

Prikhodko made it clear the presidents will discuss the Iranian nuclear problem among other issues. 'Putin's meeting with Ahmadinejad will focus on issues of bilateral cooperation including the fuel and energy sphere, the development of Caspian resources, transportation and transport corridors, as well as Russia's participation in the solution of Iranian energy problems', Prikhodko added.

'It is planned that some international issues will be discussed as well, such as the talks over the development of the Iranian peaceful nuclear program and the situation around Iraq', the aide said.

Meanwhile, major powers will coax Iran on the nuclear offer at IAEA. The powers—the five UNSC permanent members plus Germany—hoped a debate on Thursday of the IAEA's governing board would help persuade Iran to accept their offer.

'We will be keeping our statements to the board low-key to encourage Iran to come up with a positive response', said a EU3 group diplomat. Iranian foreign minister Manouchehr Mottaki told his Italian counterpart the offer was 'a significant change of approach toward Iran.'

AFP Agencies

BIBLIOGRAPHY

BP Statistical Review of World Energy, 2005. 'BRIC Ascendant—Wall St Hype vs Reality', posted on the Web by Paris, Jerome A. on 26 February 2005.

Capon, N. and W. Vanhonacker. 1999. *The Asian Marketing Casebook*, Singapore: Prentice Hall.

Cavusgil, S.T., P. Ghauri and M. Agarwal. 2002. *Doing Business in Emerging Markets*, New Delhi: Sage Publications.

'Cindia, la sfida del secolo', *Limes, Rivista Italiana di Geopolitica*, September 2005.

Dun and Bradstreet. 2006. *India in Perspective*, February and May.

Goleman, Daniel. 1995. *Emotional Intelligence*, Bantam.

Gregor, James Mc. 2005. *One Billion Customers: Lessons from the Front Lines of Doing Business in China*, New York: Free Press.

Hendon, D.W. 2001. *Classic Failures in Product Marketing*, Malaysia: Hardknocks Factory.

Hooke, J.C. 2001. *Emerging Markets: A Practical Guide for Corporations, Lenders, and Investors*, New York: Wiley and Sons.

Kotler, P., S.H. Ang and S.M. Leong, C.T. Tan. 1999. *Marketing Management, An Asian Perspective* (2nd edition), Singapore: Prentice Hall.

Landi, Claudio. 2004. *Buongiorno Asia: I nuovi giganti e la crisi dell' unilateralismo americano*, Florence: Vallecchi.

Lasserre, P. and H. Schutte. 1995. *Strategies for Asia Pacific*, London: McMillan Press.

Leonnet, J.P. and H.D. Hennessey. 1995. *Global Marketing Strategies*, Boston: Houghton Mifflin.

Pacek, N. and Daniel Thorniley. 2004. *Emerging Markets, Lessons for Business Success and the Outlook for Different Markets*.

Porter, M.E. 1980. *Competitive Strategy*, New York: The Free Press.
Rampini, Federico. 2006. *L'impero di Cindia. Cina, India e dintorni: La superpotenza asiatica da tre miliardi e metto di persone*. Milan: Mondadori.
Sachs, Goldman. 2006. *The World and the BRICs Dream*. New York: Goldman Sachs.

Periodicals

Asia Times online, Maitra, R. 'China's Shadow Over India's US Lobby', 13 September 2005.
Asia Times online, Seldin, R. 'The US Finger on China's Pulse', 16 June 2006.
Asia Times online, Bhadrakumar, M.K. 'China and Russia Embrace the Shanghai Spirit', 16 June 2006.
BBC World Business Report, 25 May 2005.
BCG, 'The New Global Challengers', May 2006.
Danmark's Nationalbank Monetary Review, Janson, T.M. and J.A.R. Larsen. 'The BRIC Countries', 2004, 4th quarter.
Economist, 'A Survey on Wealth and Philanthropy', 25 February 2006.
Economist, 'Not Very Slick', 3 December 2005.
Economist, 'Somalia Calling', 24 December 2005.
Engdahl, F.W. 'US Outflanked in Eurasia Energy Politics', on www.Atimes.com, 10 June 2006.
Financial Express, Mumbai, Maira, A. 'The Prevalent Concept of CSR Seems Stuck', 22 January 2006.
Financial Times, Guerrera, Francesco and John Burton, 'Credit Suisse Set To Create 900 Outsourced Jobs in Singapore', 11 May 2006.
Financial Times, Yeh, A. and F. Harvey, 'China Learns of Pollutant Perils as the Mercury Rises', 13 July 2006.
Harvard Business Review, Earley, P.C. and E. Rosokowath. 'Cultural Intelligence', October 2004.
Harvard Business Review, Prahalad C.K. and K. Lieberthal. 'The End of Corporate Imperialism'. 1998.
Harvard Business Review, Arnold, D.J. and John Quelch. 'New Strategies in Emerging Markets', *Harvard Business Review,* October 1998.

Hindu, 'India, China Agree to Share Experiences and Hold Consultations on Financial Sector', 9 April 2006.

Hindu, Suryanarayana, P.S. 'India May Expand Economic Pact', 9 April 2006.

Internazionale, Rome, December 2005.

Moscow Times, 'Wal-Mart Grows Bold In China', Reuters, 21 March 2006.

Pelle, S. 2004. 'Global and Local Brands', *Pearl of Wisdom*, Vol. 2, Pune: SCMHRD.

PINR, 'Intelligence Brief: Shanghai Cooperation Organization', M.A. Weinstein, 12 July 2005.

'State of the World 2006', Worldwatch Institute, Edizioni Ambiente (a cura di Gianfranco Bologna), Milan, 2006.

Time, 'Graph: Forging Ahead, on Steel Consumption', 13 February 2006.

Time, Israely, J. 'Europe Found Itself Unprepared', 5 December 2005.

Times of India, Onishi, N. 'Japan Looks for Dragon Heart', 6 June 2006.

Time, Spaeth, A. 'China's Toxic Shock', 5 December 2006.

Websites

Global Economic Website. Sachs, Goldman. *Dreaming with BRICs: The Path to 2050.* https://www.gs.com

——, BRIC's Model Projections. http://www.gs.com

Hang seng bank Limited. http://www.hangseng.com

National Intelligence Council on CIA website

Tsepko, Josephinn. 2006. 'Halls Vita C in the Ghanian Market', posted on the Web on 9 March.

UNDP Human Development Report. 2003. http://www.hdr.undp.org

http://www.transparency.org

http://www.timesfoundation.com

http://www.theodora.com (indicated source CIA WORLD FACT BOOK, 2005)

http://www.thehindu.com

http://www.uschina.org

http://www.asia-europe-network.org

http://www.bjreview.com.cn
http://www.Finfacts.com/brands.htm
http://www.osw.waw.pl
http://www.freerepublic.com
http://www.issb.co.uk
http://www.danone.com
http://bwnt.businessweek.com/brand/2005/index.asp
http://www.doingbusiness.org/exploretopics/startingbusiness

ABOUT THE AUTHOR

Stefano Pelle is Vice President and Chief Operating Officer, Business Unit Russia and South Asia, Perfetti Van Melle Group, and Chairman of Perfetti Van Melle, India. He has been living and working in South Asia since 1998, having worked previously in several MNCs, including Johnson & Johnson and Danone. He has had extensive experience in the FMCG and services sector, both in developing and in emerging countries. Before joining the Perfetti Van Melle Group, he headed the High Speed Division of the Italian State Railways. In recognition of his work in South Asia, he was made a Knight Commander by the President of the Italian Republic in 2006.